Cambridge Wizard Student Guide

The Kite Runner

By Khaled Hosseini

Sue Sherman

B.A., Dip. Ed, P. Grad Dip. (Eng)

CAMBRIDGE UNIVERSITY PRESS
Cambridge, New York, Melbourne, Madrid, Cape Town, Singapore, São Paulo

Cambridge University Press
477 Williamstown Road, Port Melbourne, VIC 3207, Australia

www.cambridge.edu.au
Information on this title: www.cambridge.edu.au/0521682347

First published 2006
Reprinted 2008

Cover design by Jeromy Jones
Typeset by Kath Puxty
Printed in Australia by Print Impressions

National Library of Australia Cataloguing in Publication data
Sherman, Sue, 1946– .
The kite runner.
For VCE English students.
ISBN-13 978-0-521-68234-3 paperback
ISBN-10 0-521-68234-7 paperback
1. Hosseini, Khaled The kite runner. I. Title.
(Series : Cambridge wizard student guide).
813.6

ISBN-13 978-0-521-68234-3 paperback
ISBN-10 0-521-68234-7 paperback

Contents

Notes on the Author

Details of Hosseini's life

Khaled Hosseini was born in Kabul, Afghanistan, in 1965. His mother was a teacher; his father a diplomat. His family left Afghanistan for a posting in Paris in 1976, well before the Communist coup and the Soviet invasion. They had every intention of returning. However, when Soviet tanks rolled into Afghanistan in 1980, the Hosseini family sought political asylum in the United States. Khaled Hosseini now lives in California, where he works as a doctor. He is married and has two children. *The Kite Runner* is his first book.

Links between author and main character

In a recent interview, Hosseini states: 'The story line of my novel is largely fictional. The characters were invented and the plot imagined. However, there certainly are, as is always the case with fiction, autobiographical elements woven through the narrative. Probably the passages most resembling my own life are the ones in the US, with Amir and Baba trying to build a new life. I, too, came to the US as an immigrant and I recall vividly those first few years in California, the brief time we spent on welfare, and the difficult task of assimilating into a new culture. My father and I did work for a while at the flea market and there really are rows of Afghans working there, some of whom I am related to.' (Razeshta Sethna: E-mail: newsline@cyber.net.pk).

Hosseini's memories of Afghanistan

Hosseini 'wanted to write about Afghanistan before the Soviet war because that is largely a forgotten period in modern Afghan history. For many people in the west, Afghanistan is synonymous with the Soviet war and the Taliban.' He explains: 'I wanted to remind people that Afghans had managed to live in peaceful anonymity for decades, that the history of the Afghans in the twentieth century has been largely peaceful and harmonious.'

Hosseini experienced Kabul with his brother 'the way Amir and Hassan do: long school days in the summer, kite fighting in the winter time, westerns with John Wayne at Cinema Park, big parties at our house in Wazir Akbar Khan, picnics in Paghman.' He has 'very fond memories of childhood in Afghanistan, largely because [his] memories, unlike those of the current generation of Afghans, are untainted by the spectre of war, landmines, and famine.' (Newsline Publications 2001).

Notes on Genre, Structure and Style

Genre

The multiple strands of the text

The Kite Runner is a complex novel – at once a 'coming of age' story, an immigrant saga and, perhaps especially, a story of moral challenge. It is also a powerful study of the bloody troubles in Afghanistan – thus a type of historical or political novel. All of these strands are analysed at length in the commentaries and theme notes which follow.

The novel is not an autobiography

While Hosseini has plainly used his own experiences as source material, it is important to understand that it is *not* an autobiography. The characters are imagined, though the setting is real. His narrator, Amir, is a fully developed individual and not in any way to be confused with the author. Both Amir's good qualities and his bad are exposed, and much of the power of the novel comes from this portrait. It is because Amir is so believable, and the author so skilled in storytelling, that we are drawn easily into his world. As with all engrossing stories, we forget the fiction and immerse ourselves in this 'reality' which, in so many ways, connects with our own experiences, leading us to reflect on our lives and our values. However, the world created by Hosseini is entirely disconnected from the experiences of many western readers and, as such, provides fascinating and often disturbing insights into a different culture.

First person narrative – the voice of Amir throughout

The novel is a first person narrative, in which the narrator is a player. It is the voice of Amir which constructs the characters (including himself) and the events of the story. Thus we are subtly positioned by *his* way of seeing, thinking and feeling. His preoccupations – as with his seemingly cold father – and his attitudes (as in his championing of Sohrab in the face of Farid's racist jibe), come across strongly. We have the sense, at times, of being trapped within the mental world of this individual. Although it might be at times claustrophobic, as when he behaves so badly, and feels so guilty, it is also a clever strategy, for it foregrounds the moral issues being considered. We have no escape from Amir, or from his ethical dilemma. Hosseini keeps our attention on that throughout. Our attitudes towards the narrator are necessarily complex. We can sympathise with him, even while we condemn his disloyalty and cowardice, as he himself does. Through his reflective and self-reflective narrative, readers are invited to endorse Hosseini's celebration of friendship and to affirm a need for trust, loyalty and moral responsibility; we are also positioned to condemn to racism, violence and the relentless pursuit of power.

Characters and their link to key themes

As is characteristic of traditional western narrative fiction, the characters embody themes. The story of Amir and Hassan, bound by brotherhood but separated by class and ethnicity is, on a larger scale, a story about universal brotherhood, and suggests that the social, political and religious boundaries that divide people can be transcended. Given the deep and enduring ethnic divisions between the Sunni and the Shi'a in Afghanistan, the book is also a quasi-political treatise.

Since the publication of *The Kite Runner,* Hosseini has received many e-mails from Afghans in exile in the US, who thank him for writing the book. He explains that 'they feel a slice of their story has been told by one of their own.' Yet there are those who have called the book divisive and objected to some of the issues raised in the book, namely 'racism, discrimination and ethnic inequality.' Hosseini argues, however, that 'if [his] book generates any sort of dialogue among Afghans, then … it will have done a service to the community.'

Structure

Mainly a chronological time scheme

The novel's narrative structure is conventional in that it follows a chronological time scheme, though with considerable jumps between relevant periods. The story itself begins with a leisurely exposition (Amir's childhood with Hassan and Baba), leading to the first major dramatic climax (Hassan's rape). At that point, the narrative appears to drift sideways – becoming momentarily a type of immigrant story. It is only many chapters (and years) later that the consequences of that earlier event reemerge, with Amir's trip to Pakistan and Afghanistan. Then the pace picks up rapidly, so much so that for a while *The Kite Runner* almost reads like a thriller, so breathless and dramatic are the events. At this point, the moral issues sidelined earlier are seen again in their full intensity, and the actions of the protagonist work to resolve them satisfactorily. The novel ends where it began (2001), in the present – the time of Amir's final redemption.

Echoes and repetitions in the text

It is worth noting that Hosseini enjoys connecting people and events. This is a novel with a very consciously crafted structure. The way Baba treats both Amir and Hassan as 'sons', which at first seems good natured, is much much later revealed to be what it actually is – the love of a father for a legitimate and an illegitimate son. The rape of Hassan echoes later both the rape of Kamal and the (implied) rape of Sohrab. The disappearance of Sanaubar seems a throwaway plot detail although when she reappears in the narrative, it is a vital reconnecting, and an echo of Hassan's forgiveness of Amir. Assef likewise disappears, only to reappear in a more despicable form at a climactic moment. The unfinished business of the day (Hassan threatened to make him 'one eyed Assef') is unwittingly finished by his son – a connection which might perhaps strain credibility but certainly delivers a very satisfying symbolism. The fathering of Amir and Hassan by Baba (and Ali) is replicated in the fathering of Sohrab by Amir.

Symbols and motifs

So much in the novel is made up of patterns like this. Like an Afghan carpet, the story's colours and shapes are reproduced many times. Symbols and motifs recur frequently. There are the kite scenes – evoking happiness and a sense of liberation. There are the scenes of blood – particularly the rape scene, the execution scene, the beating of Amir by Assef and the attempted suicide of Sohrab – all strongly evoking the cruelties and evil of life. There is the 'hare lip' – first in Hassan and then in Amir – both redolent of the theme of suffering. There is the eye of Assef – the first time threatened – the second time removed. What this means in the novel's subtext is left unexplained, though it might have something to do with Assef's one-eyed and jaundiced view of life. One can even make out an argument that Assef is the

A doppelganger?

doppelganger of Assef – his evil twin (the commentary picks this up for your consideration). There is the pomegranate tree, where they carved their names in friendship, and where later Amir betrayed his friend. Finally there is the smile. In Hassan, it is the symbol of his goodness and joy. In the battered polaroid photo, both Hassan and Sohrab are smiling. In the final scene of the novel, Sohrab is smiling once again. All these patterns bind the narrative, and give it meaning. It is part of what makes the story so satisfying.

Style

Hosseini's use of language is often highly descriptive, filled with colourful details of everyday life in Afghanistan and America. The reflective tone of the narrative constantly reminds us that this is a retrospective, and that childhood events are reconstructed through the self-critical eyes of an adult who has come to realise that, no matter how deeply you bury it, 'the past claws its way out.'

The voice of Amir

The prominent voice is Amir's, and rather shrewdly, Hosseini has chosen a highly articulate man as his narrator. Amir becomes a professional writer. Thus his moments of descriptive excitement, and of intense moral doubt, become plausible (as they would not in a less linguistically gifted individual). We can readily accept the eloquence of his style, for it is what we would expect.

Occasionally, we hear other voices – most notably in the letter from Hassan, and in the chapter 'voiced' by Rahim Khan. These provide an interesting and perhaps welcome contrast to the voice of Amir. Dialogue is used extensively, and indeed we have the differing voices of all the characters. Hosseini's skill as a writer brings all of his characters vividly to life through their dialogue.

Imagery used to create realism

Hosseini uses description as he needs to. There is vivid sensory imagery to capture the appearance and the atmosphere of his childhood home, the flea market, and the devastated city of Kabul. His use of metaphor is sparse but effective. Most notable is the pair of kites, symbolising the friendship of Amir and Hassan, and a need to transcend social and ethnic boundaries to forge bonds of brotherhood. Yet at other times, he pulls back, quite properly. He could have described both the rape and the execution in nauseating detail, but he does not. The reason is that in such cases imagining is often far more powerful (and more discreet) than a graphic description. One of the most important sentences in the text is just two words long, and contains only one noun: 'A smile.' Like all serious writers, he uses words as he needs to, varying their intensity from moments of high passion to others of gentle reflection. Hosseini's carefully crafted writing allows us to enjoy the text on a literary, as well as a narrative level.

Background Notes

A Brief History of Afghanistan

Afghanistan is often called the 'crossroads of Central Asia.' A landlocked, arid country, high in the Himalayas, sharing borders with Iran, Uzbekistan, Tajikistan, China and Pakistan. It is also sometimes categorised within South Asia and the Middle East. For millennia, it has seen merchants, pilgrims and warlords traversing its lands. It is a poor country. Even today its 24 million people have a GDP per capita of only $US 784 (opposed to Australia's $20,000) and an average life expectancy of 45 years (Australia's is 78).

Ancient history of the country

It has had a turbulent history. In 328 BC, Alexander the Great entered the territory of present-day Afghanistan, then part of the Persian Empire. In 642 AD, Arabs invaded the entire region and introduced Islam. Genghis Khan led a successful Mongol invasion in 1219. Following his death (in 1227), a succession of petty chiefs and princes struggled for supremacy. Late in the 14th century, one of Khan's descendants, Tamerlane (Tamerlane the Great), incorporated Afghanistan into his own vast Asian empire. In 1747, a Pashtun, Ahmad Shah Durrani, established what is known today as Afghanistan.

The twentieth century

In modern times, King Amanullah (1919-29) moved to end his country's traditional isolation by establishing diplomatic relations with most major countries. He introduced several reforms intended to modernise Afghanistan. Some of these, such as the abolition of the traditional Muslim veil for women and the opening of a number of co-educational schools, quickly alienated many tribal and religious leaders. Faced with overwhelming armed opposition, Amanullah was forced to abdicate in January 1929 and Prince Nadir Khan, a cousin of Amanullah's, was declared King Nadir Shah. Four years later, however, he was assassinated by a Kabul student.

Mohammad Zahir Shah, Nadir Khan's 19-year-old son, succeeded to the throne and reigned from 1933 to 1973. Zahir's cousin, Sardar Mohammad Daoud, served as his Prime Minister from 1953 to 1963. Daoud's alleged support for the creation of a Pashtun state in the Pakistan-Afghan border area heightened tensions with

Pakistan and eventually resulted in Daoud's dismissal in March 1963.

Amid charges of corruption against the royal family and poor economic conditions created by the severe 1971–72 drought, former Prime Minister Daoud seized power in a military coup on 17 July, 1973. Zahir Shah fled the country, eventually finding refuge in Italy. Daoud abolished the monarchy and declared Afghanistan a republic with himself as its first President and Prime Minister. On 27 April, 1978, the PDPA (The People's Democratic Party of Afghanistan), a Communist faction, initiated a bloody coup known as the Great Saur Revolution, which resulted in the overthrow and murder of Daoud.

During its first eighteen months of rule, the PDPA brutally imposed a Marxist-style reform program, which ran counter to deeply-rooted Afghan traditions. In addition, thousands of members of the traditional elite, the religious establishment, and the intelligentsia were imprisoned, tortured, or murdered. Conflicts within the PDPA also surfaced early and resulted in exiles, purges, imprisonments, and executions.

The Soviet invasion

On 24 December, 1979, large numbers of Soviet airborne forces, joining thousands of Soviet troops already on the ground, began to land in Kabul under the pretext of a field exercise. An overwhelming majority of Afghans opposed the communist regime, either actively or passively. Afghan freedom fighters ('mujahideen') made it almost impossible for the regime to maintain a system of local government outside major urban centres. Poorly armed at first, in 1984 the mujahideen began receiving substantial assistance in the form of weapons and training from the US and other outside powers. This led to the Soviets withdrawel in 1989.

The Taliban

The Taliban had risen to power in the mid-1990s in reaction to the anarchy that arose after the withdrawal of Soviet forces. The name 'Taliban' is from the Pashtun and Persian word for 'those who study the book,' and signifies students of the Koran. Its founding spiritual leader, mullah (priest) Mohammed Omar of Kandahar, according to legend, punished a local mujahideen commander who had raped two girls, thereby initiating the movement. It is not true, but he *was* a galvanising force in the movement, which unquestionably proclaims strict Muslim principles. Many Taliban had been educated in Pakistan and were largely from rural southern Pashtun backgrounds. In 1994, the Taliban, assisted by the Pakistanis and probably with covert US funding (because they were anti-Soviet), developed enough strength to capture the city of Kandahar from a local warlord. They proceeded to expand their control throughout Afghanistan, occupying Kabul in September 1996. Despite desperate and bloody battles and many losses, by the end of 1998, the Taliban occupied about 90% of the country.

The Taliban proclaimed the 'Islamic Emirate of Afghanistan' and sought to impose the strictest form of Islam, 'Sharia.' They banned television, all forms of imagery, music and sports. A religious police force was established to enforce Sharia law. Those caught stealing could have their hands cut off. The punishment for adultery was stoning to death. They committed massive human rights violations, particularly directed against women and girls. The Taliban also committed serious atrocities against minority populations, particularly the Shi'a Hazara ethnic group. In 2001, as part of a drive against relics of Afghanistan's pre-Islamic past, the Taliban destroyed two priceless ancient Buddha statues carved into cliff faces outside of the city of Bamiyan. Ironically, given the title of this book, amongst the many things they banned was kite flying!

Position of women

The vast majority of Afghanistan's population professes to follow Islam. Over 1400 years ago, Islam asserted that men and women were equal before God, and gave them various rights such as the right to inheritance, the right to vote, the right to work, and even choose their own partners in marriage. However, for centuries in Afghanistan, women had been denied these rights either by official government decree or by their own husbands, fathers, and brothers.

During the rule of the Taliban (1996 – 2001), women were forbidden to work, to attend schools or universities, to leave the house without a male escort, to seek medical help from a male doctor, to wear cosmetics or high heeled shoes, to play sport, to ride bicycles or motorbikes, to wear brightly coloured clothes, to appear on balconies, to be photographed or filmed, even to travel on the same bus as men. They were forced to cover themselves from head to toe, even covering their eyes. Women who were doctors and teachers were suddenly forced to be beggars and even prostitutes in order to feed their families.

Bin Laden

From the mid-1990s the Taliban provided sanctuary to Osama Bin Laden. In return, Bin Laden provided both financial and political support to the Taliban. Bin Laden and his al-Qaeda group were charged with the bombing of the US Embassies in Nairobi and Dar es Salaam in 1998. In August 1998, the US launched a cruise missile attack against Bin Laden's terrorist camp in south eastern Afghanistan. Bin Laden and al-Qaeda have acknowledged their responsibility for the September 11, 2001 terrorist attacks against the United States.

Shi'a history

The term Shi'a (or Shi'ite) derives from a shortening of Shi'at Ali or partisans of Ali. Ali is the central figure at the origin of the Shi'a / Sunni split which occurred in the decades immediately following the death of the Prophet in 632. Shi'a's feel that Ali should have been the first caliph and that the caliphate should pass down only to direct descendants of Mohammed; however, a rival claimant, Yazid, succeeded to the caliphate. Ali's younger son, Hussein, led an army against Yazid but, hopelessly outnumbered, he and his men were slaughtered at the Battle of Karbala (in modern day Iraq), which set in place the significance of martyrdom for the Shi'a and consolidated divisions between the Shi'a and what came to be known as the Sunni.

The Pashtuns and the Hazaras

Hazaras are one of the most oppressed and dispossessed national minority ethnic groups of Afghanistan and, because they are clearly distinguishable from other ethnic groups, easily victimised. Most Hazaras (like Hassan) have broad faces with flat noses and narrow eyes, scant facial hair, and are shorter and smaller in build than the other ethnic groups in Afghanistan. Historically, the reason for this is malnutrition. To eradicate Hazara ethnic identity and consolidate Pashtun domination, the ruling circle in Afghan, influenced by the Nazi ideology and the rise of Germany as a major world power, continued the Pashtunization of every aspect of non-Pashtun ethnic society. The character of Assef, in *The Kite Runner* exemplifies this chilling aspect of Pashtun ideology Hazaras were subjected to all kinds of public humiliation and embarrassment and taunted by derogatory terms such as Hazara-e-mushkur (mice-eating Hazaras), bini puchuq (flat-nose), khar-e-barkash (load-carrying donkey), etc. In The *Kite Runner,* both Hassan and his father, Ali, are subjected to this form of racial vilification.

Sources: Rauf Zeerak. 'The Hazaras and their role in Afghanistan' http://www.hazara.com/article/role_of_hazaras_part1.pdf

Richter Adam. 'A Brief History of Afghanistan'

http://www.afghangovernment.com/briefhistory.htm

Advice on the accuracy of historical information from the Internet was given by Dr Shahram Akbarzadeh (Senior Lecturer in Global Politics, Monash University) and Assoc. Professor Constant J. Mews, (Director, Centre for Studies in Theology, Monash University), and is gratefully acknowledged.

Storyboard Synopsis

The storyboard below offers a quick reference synopsis of *The Kite Runner*.

For full details of what happens in each chapter, refer to the full synopsis and commentary which follows (pages 15–55).

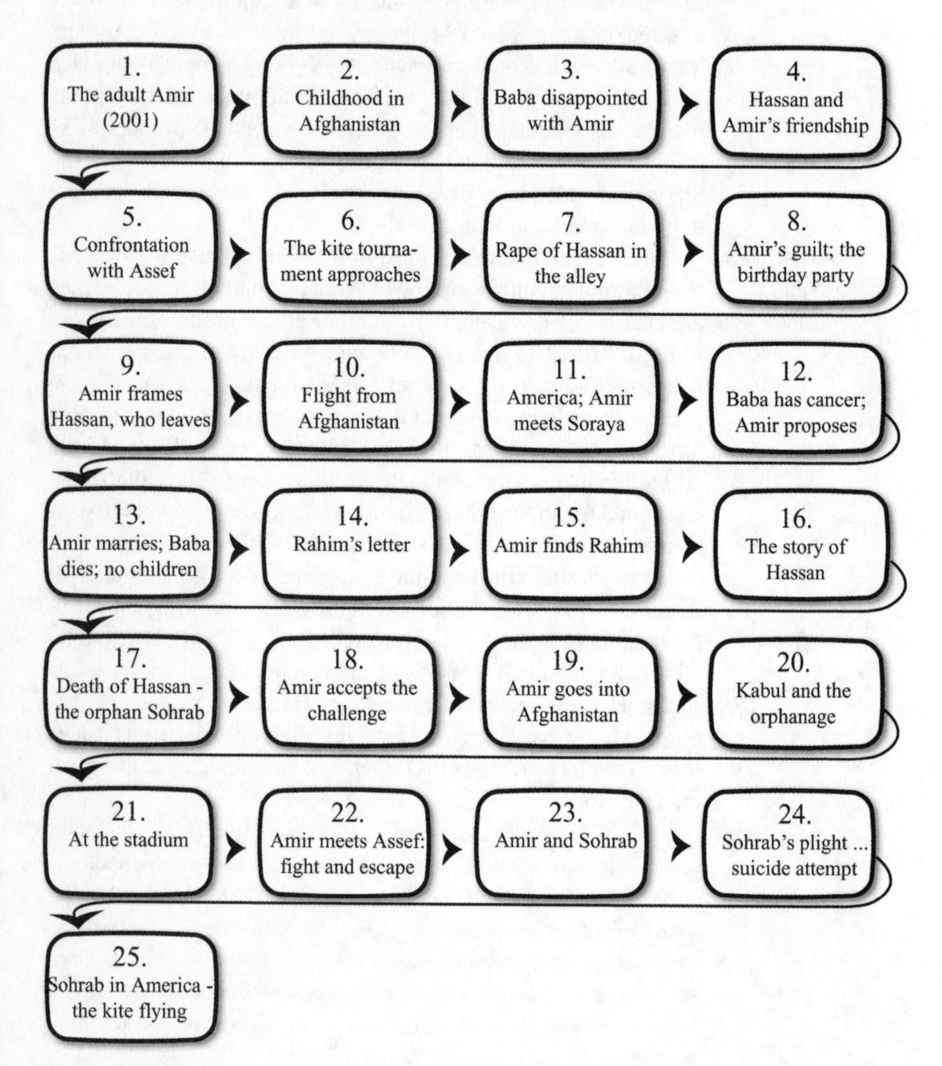

Summary and Commentary

Chapter One

The legacy of the past

The narrator, Amir, is an adult in San Francisco. He is watching kites being flown. Suddenly his childhood is recalled, **'my past of unatoned sins.'** He thinks of the moment in the winter of 1975 when, at the age of 12, his life changed forever. Amir clearly remembers the precise moment in an alley long ago – a life-changing incident, which, we are led to assume, will be the subject of the narrative. We are also briefly introduced to Hassan, whose voice 'whispers' in [Amir's] head:

Quote

For you, a thousand times over. Hassan the hare-lipped kite runner.

Commentary

A pair of kites 'floating side by side' in the sky over the Golden Gate Park evoke the sound of Hassan's voice and introduce two of the text's major themes: friendship (Hassan) and redemption (the 'unatoned sins'). This brief juxtaposition of past and present and the contrasts between America and Afghanistan, alert readers to the oppositions of time and place which will underpin the narrative.

Chapter Two

Amir's early childhood

An idyllic childhood is remembered by Amir. He is a Pashtun (member of the dominant tribe in Afghanistan), and the only child of a wealthy and powerful businessman (Baba). Amir spends his days playing with Hassan, the hare-lipped son of his father's lower caste Hazara servant (Ali). The two boys are close friends but Hassan idolises Amir, obeying his every wish.

Quote

Hassan never denied me anything.

Amir and Hassan's relationship

He even accepts the blame when the boys incur disapproval for minor transgressions. Amir and Hassan are both motherless, Amir's mother having died giving birth to him and Hassan's having abandoned him a week after his birth. Ali would remind the boys that **'there was a brotherhood between people who had fed from the same breast [the wet nurse] a kinship that not even time could break.**' Amir's first word is *Baba*. Hassan's is *Amir*.

Amir grieves silently for his beautiful and well-educated mother (a Pashtun 'princess' whose life was 'sacrificed' to produce a son), Hassan, by contrast, lives with the burden of his mother's shame. Sanaubar, a beautiful Hazara woman was seen as a temptress and coerced into an unsuitable marriage with an older man to salvage family honour. She is never spoken of by her husband and son and condemned by society as a 'dishonourable' woman.

The young Amir idolises and fears his father, Baba. However, it is his father's best friend and business partner, Rahim Khan, whose finger the infant Amir grasps in the family photo. As he grows older, Amir sometimes begs to be included in after-dinner discussions with Baba's guests, but is always told that it's 'grown-ups' time.'

Commentary

The theme of brotherhood is established from the outset with the two motherless infants having the same wet nurse. The first words spoken by each reveal what is most important to them, and lay the 'foundations for what happened in 1975' – and 'all that followed.' This theme is to be a vital part of the novel's moral fabric. Amir's sense of connection to Afghanistan will largely, though not entirely, be associated with his ambivalent feelings for his old childhood friend.

Another key idea is Amir's sense of unworthiness. Baba's wealth and power is established in the description of his house: 'the most beautiful house in the ... district.' Baba entertains lavishly and always prefers the company of his friends to that of his son. The tone of subdued regret with which Amir describes himself, outside the closed doors of his father's study, sitting sometimes for two hours, listening to the chatter and laughter, shows the young boy's yearning for affection and acceptance.

Chapter Three

Baba's power and success

Baba's nickname is 'Mr Hurricane'. He is reputed to have wrestled a black bear and has the scars to prove it, adding much credibility to his powerful mystique. He is the centre of attention at any gathering and delights in taking on challenges in order to prove to critics and sceptics that he is capable of achieving whatever goal he sets himself, be it marrying a princess, succeeding in business or building an orphanage.

One day, Amir returns from his Islamic school to tell Baba that his drinking is a sin. Baba dismisses the mullahs as 'self-righteous monkeys' and tells Amir:

Quote

> Now, no matter what the mullah teaches, there is only one sin, only one. And that is theft. Every other sin is a variation of theft .... When you kill a man, you steal a life...You steal his wife's right to a husband, rob his children of a father. When you tell a lie, you steal someone's right to the truth. When you cheat, you steal the right to fairness. Do you see?

Amir valiantly endeavours to measure up to his father's expectations. However, he is a studious child with no talent for or interest in soccer (Baba's passion). Amir's ineffectual attempts to impress, or even interest his father, seem doomed to failure. Baba seems more responsive to Ali's son. Amir is jealous, and excludes Hassan from the trip to the lake so that he can have Baba to himself.

Amir's jealousy

In an attempt to make Amir more like a 'real boy', Baba signs Amir up for a soccer team but Amir is a 'pathetic, blundering liability'. He takes Amir to a *chapandaz*, a rough and dangerous game involving horseback riders battling for possession of an animal carcass. Amir is so distressed at the sight of a fallen rider, trampled and bloodied, that, much to his father's undisguised disgust, Amir cries 'all the way back home'. Amir subsequently overhears Baba confiding in Rahim Khan about his disappointment with his son, and Amir knows that at the heart of Baba's rejection of him is death of his beloved wife during his birth.

Amir upset by violence

Commentary

Baba seems invincible to his awestruck son. Amir describes Baba as a 'force of nature', a 'towering' giant, whose 'thundering' presence was, like 'the sun', capable of turning the heads of sunflowers. Amir's overwhelming sense of insignificance is intensified by such a father and exceeds the ordinary feelings of awe that many young boys feel for their fathers. Amir's fear of his father, his fierce pride in Baba's achievements and his own desperate longing for acceptance, underpin a mutually unsatisfying relationship, for which Amir almost entirely blames himself. Only Rahim Khan can see fault in Baba, who cannot accept a son who is not an image of his own success and power.

Chapter Four

Ali's history

Ali's parents were Hazaras (an Afghan ethnic minority), killed in a road accident by wealthy Pashtun brothers. Amir's grandfather, a 'highly regarded judge', sentenced the brothers to military service and adopted into his own household the couple's orphaned son, Ali. Foreshadowing the relationship of Ali and Hassan, Ali, is the childhood playmate of Baba. Like his son, Hassan, Ali also has a physical disability: he is crippled with polio.

Ali and Hassan's friendship

Amir remembers an idyllic childhood. Hassan's deadly accuracy with the slingshot is noted as a feature of their boyhood adventures. However while Amir eats breakfast, Hassan makes Amir's bed, polishes his shoes, irons his clothes and packs his schoolbag. Amir reads to Hassan (who is illiterate). Hassan is entranced with the stories. His favourite one is about a Persian hero who mortally wounds his own son without knowing who he is. The son's dying words include:

Quote

> If thou are indeed my father, then hast thou stained thy sword in the life-blood of thy son. And thou didst it of thine obstinacy. For I sought to turn thee unto love … But I appealed unto thy heart in vain …

Amir finds that Hassan is so much quicker at solving riddles that he stops reading them. Amir recognises his arrogance in mocking Hassan's 'ignorance', and tries to convince himself later (unsuccessfully) that his behaviour is a 'harmless prank'.

Responses to Amir's story

Hassan enthusiastically praises a story which Amir has embellished and buoyed by his success, Amir writes a story which he offers to his father for approval. However, Baba's 'thin smile' and 'feigned interest' are devastating, and Rahim Khan is forced to 'rescue' Amir by offering to read the story. Humiliated and angry, Amir wishes he could 'open [his] veins and drain [Baba's] cursed blood from his body.'

Ali generously bestows on Amir the praise he desperately needs, informing him that God has granted him a 'special talent' acknowledging his gift for 'irony'. Jubilant, Amir reads the story to Hassan, who responds enthusiastically, yet asks an innocent question which entirely undermines the development of Amir's plot.

Commentary

The theme of friendship is explored through the relationships between Baba and Ali and, in the next generation, between their sons, Amir and Hassan. These friendships are complicated by ethnic and class differences between the Pashtun (Sunni) ruling class (Baba and Amir) and the Hazara (Shi'a) lower class (Ali and Hassan). Although they are bound by genuine affection to their childhood friends, Baba and Amir never forget their ethnic superiority. Amir reflects that in none of the stories he ever told about his childhood exploits with Ali, did Baba 'ever refer to Ali as a friend'. Without a trace of irony, Amir admits that 'the curious thing was, [he] never thought of Hassan and [himself] as friends either'. Amir takes Hassan's devotion entirely for granted and mocks his friend's illiteracy, partly because he is uncomfortably aware that his uneducated servant is in many ways, much cleverer than he is. Sadly, despite their friendships, it seems as if 'nothing' can ever 'overcome' an entrenched historical hierarchy in which Hazara inferiority is deemed to be an inescapable fact of life.

Amir's painful relationship with his father continues to be a major theme. The Persian tale (quoted p.18) is an oblique reference to it, insofar as in both, proud and disdainful fathers cause terrible harm to their sons. Ironically, however, that same arrogance and disdain becomes one of Amir's own defining characteristics in his relationship with Hassan, who is in very much the same supplicant position to him as he is to Baba. The author does not remark on this, for obvious reasons, but it is there in the subtext as another thread in the novel's moral argument.

Chapter Five

The King is overthrown

The sound of gunfire heralds the 'bloodless' coup which ends the forty year reign of King Zahir Shah and installs his cousin Daoud Khan. Terrified by the gunfire, Hassan is comforted by his father, who pulls him close and 'clutch[es] him with tenderness'. Amir notes, **'Later, I would tell myself that I hadn't felt envious of Hassan. Not at all.'** which suggests quite the opposite. Baba's concern is expressed when he returns, but he embraces Amir, Hassan *and* Ali. The following morning, the people of Kabul awake to find that the monarchy is 'a thing of the past'.

Assef bullies Amir and Hassan

On one of their walks together, Amir and Hassan are confronted by a local thug, Assef, who insults Hassan and hurls a stone at him. Assef is a tall, blond-haired bully who arms himself with brass knuckles and surrounds himself with a sycophantic gang. Assef criticises Amir for his friendship with a 'dirty' Hazara, and states:

Quote

Afghanistan is the land of the Pashtuns. It always has been, always will be. We are the true Afghans, the pure Afghans, not this Flat-Nose here. His people pollute our homeland ... they dirty our blood.

As Assef slips on his brass knuckles and prepares to punish Amir for his degrading friendship, Hassan arms himself with his deadly slingshot and, despite his fear, courageously confronts Assef. Furious and humiliated, Assef backs down, but warns both Amir and Hassan that he will take revenge.

Hassan's lip is repaired

Hassan's birthday is celebrated, as it is every year, with a gift from Baba. This year it is the gift of an operation to repair Hassan's hare-lip. Amir comments (from his adult perspective) that ironically, just as the permanent 'smile' of his facial deformity is surgically repaired, the events of the following winter completely eradicate Hassan's ability to smile.

Commentary

Apart from more insights into the fraught relationship of Amir and Baba, this chapter is notable as his first major moral challenge. It is the psychotic and vicious Assef, a contemptible thug with a taste for ethnic cleansing, who confronts Amir with his own cowardice and disloyalty. In the face of Assef's aggression, the timid Amir says nothing to defend his Hazara friend. Unwilling to risk physical harm, he abandons the ties of years and assures Assef that Hassan is not his 'friend', merely his 'servant'. In stark contrast, Hassan's loyalty and courage are unquestioned and he defends Amir in the face of overwhelming odds. It is even more laudable in the face of Amir's betrayal. Significantly, Hassan never reproaches Amir and unquestioningly accepts his inferior status. However, the author has clearly made a point about who has acted properly, and who has not.

Chapter Six

The kite tournament

Kites provide a 'paper-thin slice of intersection' between the 'different spheres of existence' inhabited by Amir and Hassan. Recognising that Amir's and Hassan's talents are more suited to the strategic battles of the tournament than the construction of the kites, Baba buys them the best kites at a specialist kite maker. Amir's considerable skill as a kite fighter is immeasurably enhanced by these kites and by Hassan's uncanny ability as a kite runner. Yet Amir's wealth and privelege are also significant factors in his success.

The participants in the annual kite tournament compete to keep their kites airborne – the last kite to fall is declared the winner. When the kites are cut from the string, the kite runners chase them through the streets to claim the coveted prize: the last fallen kite of the winter tournament. It is a 'trophy of honour'.

As they practise for the final tournament, and wait for a kite to fall to earth, Amir half-playfully tests Hassan's loyalty, enquiring whether he would '**Eat dirt if I told you to.**' A searching look passes

Amir and Hassan argue

between the two friends and Amir senses another side of Hassan, '**another, a second face, this one lurking just beneath the surface**'. Suddenly, the kite drops into Hassan's outstretched arms. Amir's higher social standing is rendered almost meaningless as the forces of nature deliver the kite to Hassan.

Preparation for last tournament

Excitement and tension increase in the district as the final tournament draws near. Baba takes an unprecedented interest in Amir, confidently predicting that he will win. Amir is almost overwhelmed by the force of Baba's expectations, dreading the possibility of not measuring up and, at the same time, basking in the glow of an imagined victory. This, he speculates, might finally earn him a pardon: '**maybe I would finally be pardoned for killing my mother.**'

Commentary

Amir's test of Hassan's loyalty is another sign of his arrogance (as member of the Pashtun elite), as well as his insecurity. Why, we wonder, does he constantly need to exert power over the obviously powerless Hassan? Because of his own feelings of inadequacy, of course. Yet, even as Hassan verbally confirms his absolute loyalty to Amir, there is that telling look. 'Beneath the surface' of his gaze, Hassan implicitly asserts that bonds of brotherhood cancel out racial and class divisions. The kites floating high above the divided city of Kabul serve as an appropriate metaphor for Hassan's transcendent view of friendship.

Chapter Seven

The day of the tournament

Amir awakes on the morning of the tournament, anxious about letting his father down yet again. As dozens of kites fill the morning sky, the cutting of the strings starts and the first of the defeated kites begin to fall to the ground. With his own kite triumphantly aloft, Amir's gaze shifts to Baba and Rahim Khan, sitting on the rooftop to watch the tournament. Gradually, the kites' numbers dwindle to the last dozen, then to four. Amir senses the possibility of victory. He cuts down the blue kite and the crowd erupts in a frenzy of cheering. Amir has won. Baba stands and claps, '**proud of [him] at last**'. Hassan sets off to retrieve the blue kite, uttering the words that will haunt Amir for many years: '**For you a thousand times over**.'

Amir sets off to find Hassan. At the mouth of a blind alley, he comes upon Hassan and the blue kite, blocking his way out are Assef and his friends. Taking care to keep himself hidden, Amir watches as Hassan refuses to give up the kite. Hassan fires a rock from his sling shot and Assef charges at him, knocking him to the ground. The narrative is dramatically interrupted at this point with a series of Amir's memories about brotherhood, a blind fortune-teller and a dream about a snowstorm. The narrative then continues, and Assef prepares to rape Hassan. Another memory intervenes: a description of a ritual sheep slaughter. Amir is faced with a terrible choice.

Hassan is raped

Quote

I had one last chance to make a decision. One final opportuniy to decide who I was going to be. I could step into that alley, stand up for Hassan – the way he'd stood up for me all those times in the past – and accept whatever would happen to me. Or I could run. In the end, I ran.

He returns to the alley only when he knows that Assef and his friends have gone. Brutalised and humiliated, Hassan hands Amir the kite.

Quote

Did he know I knew? And if he knew, then what would I see if I *did* look in his eyes? Blame? Indignation? Or, God forbid, what I feared most: guileless devotion? That, most of all, I couldn't bear to see.

Amir, pretending not to notice Hassan's distress, returns home to savour the affection of his proud father.

Commentary

There is a dramatic irony about the kite tournament: it is simultaneously the highest and lowest point of Amir's childhood. The rape of Hassan by the despicable Assef is a scene of shocking brutality, all the more haunting because much is left to the imagination. Hassan's tears of pain afterwards, the terrible humiliation and the suspicion that Amir could/should have intervened, suggest that Amir was complicit (if only by his absence) in the atrocity.

While readers might sympathise with the insecure child, desperate for the affection of a distant and unforgiving father, we cannot condone his acts of cowardice and betrayal – and neither can Amir himself. More deeply disturbing, perhaps, is Amir's ingrained racial prejudice. From the depths of his subconscious mind emerges the thought that '**He was just a Hazara.**' The stark honesty with which Amir describes his unconscionable behaviour reveals the depth of racial intolerance in Afghanistan. If such close friends are prejudiced, what hope is there of tolerance and acceptance on a broader scale?

Structurally significant in this important chapter are the interventions of memory, interrupting the shocking narrative details. The first 'collage' of memories, which occurs as Assef knocks Hassan to the ground, reminds Amir of the bond of brotherhood which unites him with Hassan. The second recalls a blind fortune-teller, whose tactile exploration of Hassan's face reveals Hassan's ethnicity, prompting the old man to return the rupia Hassan has given him. Amir, however, withdraws his hand from the fortune-teller's, refusing him a donation and contrasting the generosity of the Hazara servant with the selfishness of the privileged Pashtun. The third memory involves a blinding snowstorm and a familiar hand reaching out for Amir. This hand symbolises Hassan, whose steadfast loyalty is the one thing that Amir can always rely on. These memories (like the racist thoughts, arise unbidden to the forefront of Amir's consciousness) indicate the path which Amir knows that he *should* choose. The final image of the sacrificial lamb is an obvious parallel with Hassan, who sacrifices himself with the same look of tragic 'resignation.'

Chapter Eight

Amir racked with guilt

Hassan seems to be avoiding Amir. He prepares Amir's breakfast and irons his clothes before Amir rises, and spends most of his time in bed. Amir evades Ali's worried questions, treating him as a troublesome servant. Amir asks Baba if they can go to Jalalabad, relishing the idea of spending time alone with Baba. Amir's pleasure is dampened by Baba's suggestion that Hassan accompany them, and his jealousy is increased by Baba's obvious concern over Hassan's health.

A trip to Jalalabad

Baba manages to invite another two dozen people and, during the journey on the bus, he cannot refrain from boasting about Amir's success. Amir's car sickness signifies his discomfort over compliments from proud aunts and uncles. The party arrives at the house of Kaka Homayoun and they enjoy a traditional feast, for which Amir has little appetite. He is so uncomfortable with the continued praise for his tournament victory that he is unable to sleep that night. He confesses aloud: '**I watched Hassan get raped**' – but no one hears him.

Amir and Hassan's friendship deteriorates

At Hassan's request, Amir and Hassan trek up their favourite hill to the pomegranate tree, and Amir is distressed by the words of friendship carved into the trunk of the tree – '***Amir* and *Hassan*: the sultans of Kabul.**'

Baba and Amir become closer but Amir is intuitively aware that Baba's newfound interest and affection will surely diminish as the tournament victory loses its gloss: '**We'd actually deceived ourselves into thinking that a toy made of tissue paper, glue and bamboo could somehow close the chasm between us.**'

Amir coldly rebuffs Hassan's attempts at communication and wallows in his own wretchedness. Hassan tactfully withdraws but his presence remains pervasive – freshly ironed clothes and cooked breakfasts signal his '**unwavering loyalty,**' sharply contrasting with Amir's shameful disloyalty.

Amir asks Baba about the possibility of 'getting new servants.' Baba's defence of Ali and Hassan is swift and unequivocal. He threatens Amir with a beating if the suggestion is ever repeated and adds, '**You bring me shame.**' The old tensions between father and son resurface. Amir is relieved when school recommences a week later.

Amir attacks Hassan

One afternoon Amir invites Hassan to go up the hill and listen to a new story he has written and Hassan eagerly agrees. Amir provokes Hassan, hurling a pomegranate at him, and insisting that Hassan hit him back. '**I wished he'd give me the punishment I craved, so maybe I'd finally sleep at night. Maybe then things could return to how they used to be between us.**' When Hassan refuses, Amir taunts him, 'pelting' him until he's exhausted. Stained with red but undaunted, Hassan demands to know, '**Are you**

satisfied? Do you feel better?'

Amir's birthday

With his usual extravagance, Baba organises Amir's birthday party and the house is filled with guests, among them Assef and his parents. Assef flatters Baba and Amir is distressed at the sight of his father 'bonding' with Assef. Amir unwillingly accepts Assef's gift. It is a biography of Hitler, which he later throws away.

Rahim Khan finds him alone. He tells Amir the story of a girl he almost married: a Hazara girl. His horrified family prevented the marriage and Rahim Khan reflects that it was '**Probably for the best, though. She would have suffered. My family would never have accepted her as an equal.**' Suddenly and inexplicably, he informs Amir that he can tell him 'anything' at any time. Amir almost does. Returning to the house for a fireworks display arranged by Baba as part of the festivities, Amir glimpses, in a burst of light, Hassan serving drinks to Assef.

Commentary

The trip to Jalalabad and the celebration of Amir's victory, only serves to increase Amir's self-loathing. His physical sickness and loss of appetite suggest that he cannot 'stomach' his own disloyalty. His confession (though unheard) and his inability to sleep indicate his guilt. He has, like Shakespeare's tragic villain, Macbeth, lost the capacity for the untroubled sleep that comes with a clear conscience.

The scene with the pomegranates, and Amir's frenzied striking out at his loyal friend is a pathetically transparent attempt to find fault with Hassan, projecting his own cowardice onto a friend whose loyalty has become unendurable. It is also of course an attempt to find the 'punishment' or payback which will cleanse him of his sin. The reflective, self-critical adult voice of the narrator clearly recognises this, and the wretched child who buries his head 'under his pillow' and cries, is also implicitly aware of his wrongdoing but unable to find a way out. His one chance of redemption and support – offered by Rahim Khan – is passed up. This, too, is a failure of nerve.

Amir's pain is exacerbated by seeing Assef welcomed into his house as a guest, and worse, smiled upon by Baba. Amir finds Baba's obvious approval of Assef galling on two counts: he is clearly the kind of son Baba would have liked, and beneath his ingratiating façade, Assef is a vicious, perverted bully. Rahim Khan seeks out Amir, seeming to understand the source of his troubles, but Amir cannot open up to him. Unable to forgive himself, he will not subject himself to the condemnation of others. Rahim Khan's story about the Hazara girl draws a subtle parallel with Amir and Hassan's friendship, reaffirming the idea that in Afghanistan, racial boundaries are impenetrable barriers. The image of Hassan and Assef together, the victim forced (by caste) to serve the criminal, is a painful reminder of Amir's own prejudice and disloyalty.

Chapter Nine

Opening his presents the next morning, Amir reflects bitterly that '**Baba would have never thrown [him] a party like that if [he] hadn't won the tournament.**' The only gift that doesn't feel like 'blood money' is Rahim Khan's leather-bound notebook – a generous affirmation of Amir's writing skills. Amir reflects on Rahim Khan's story and decides that, in order to lessen Hassan's 'suffering', he will 'have to go'. Amir plants some of the money he received for his birthday and the watch his father had given him under Hassan's mattress, and reports the 'theft' to his father.

Amir accuses Hassan

To his surprise and horror, though, when questioned by Baba, Hassan admits to the theft.

Quote

Then I understood: This was Hassan's final sacrifice for me. If he'd said no, Baba would have believed him because we all knew Hassan never lied. And if Baba believed him, then I'd be the accused … I would be revealed for what I really was.

Amir realises that Hassan knows he witnessed the rape. Baba forgives Hassan, but Ali announces that they are leaving. His coldness when he looks at Amir reveals that he, too, knows about the rape and about Amir's betrayal. Despite Baba's pleading, Ali and Hassan leave. As they depart in Baba's car, the rain begins to fall and Amir imagines that if it were a movie he would chase the car and tell Hassan he is sorry. Instead, he does nothing.

Commentary

Readers' sympathy for Amir is mightily challenged by his calculated treachery here. It is the absolute low point (morally) of Amir's journey. Again, the narrative voice offers no excuses for Amir's shameful behaviour. The image of rain suggests deep sorrow – and not only Amir's – as the close friendships forged in infancy are tragically severed by dishonesty and treachery.

Yet who is ultimately responsible for this tragic situation? Are we to blame Amir, as he himself does? To what extent can we blame Baba, whose lack of affection for and unreasonably high expectations of his son led Amir to sacrifice his friend in order to win Baba's approval? Is a society with rigidly enforced class boundaries and deeply entrenched racial prejudice largely responsible for the way that individuals behave? These questions are certainly raised by the text and need careful consideration. In arriving at 'answers', we must look closely at how the characters develop and what they ultimately learn about themselves and the world they inhabit.

Chapter Ten

Amir and Baba flee

Six years later, Amir and Baba, with a small group of refugees, hurriedly leave Afghanistan. They are with Karim, a people smuggler who runs a 'lucrative business'. Amir again embarrasses Baba by being carsick. Amir reflects on the city they have left behind. Kabul has become a dangerous place where 'grim-faced Russian soldiers' patrol the streets. The city is ruled by *rafiqs* ('comrades') who have 'split Kabul into two groups': spies, and those who are spied upon.

Baba confronts a Russian soldier

At a checkpoint, a Russian and an Afghan soldier inspect the truck. The Russian demands sexual favours from one of the occupants (a young married Afghan woman) in order to let the truck pass. Baba courageously confronts him: '**Ask him where his shame is .... Tell him I'll take a thousand of his bullets before I let this indecency take place.**' When the Russian threatens to shoot him, and draws his gun, Baba responds with his own threat: to '**tear [the Russian] to pieces**' if he misses. Amir closes his eyes. A warning shot is fired by an older Russian officer who disapproves of his younger comrade's behaviour. The young woman's husband gratefully kisses Baba's hand as the truck continues its journey towards Jalalabad.

Arrival in Jalalabad

The refugees are ushered from the truck into a small house to await the arrival of Karim's brother, Toor, who is to take them to Peshawar, but they are informed that Toor's truck has broken down. In a murderous rage, Baba nearly strangles Karim, but is prevented by the woman (whom he saved earlier). They soon discover that there are other refugees who have been waiting for two weeks. The small group from Kabul joins the refugees in the rat-infested basement, where they remain for a further week. One of the refugees is, to Amir's horror, Kamal, who was with Assef when Hassan was raped. He is strangely 'withered'. One night his father reveals to Baba that Kamal was raped during the violence of the Russian occupation.

Amir recognises Kamal

In the fuel truck

Finally some transportation is arranged but it is a fuel truck. Amir graphically describes the suffocating conditions in the fuel truck. It is pitch black and the air is thick with the stench of gasoline fumes. Only Baba's strength and encouragement enable Amir to cope with the pain of simply breathing the toxic air. They emerge at last from the stifling chamber to find themselves in Pakistan. However, Kamal has succumbed to the deadly fumes; his grief-stricken father takes Karim's gun, and turns it on himself.

Kamal dies

Commentary

The horrors of the Russian occupation are suggested in the few brief details of life in Kabul, and in Amir and Baba's desperate flight from their home.

Baba's heroic action in saving the woman is not just a dramatic incident, it also carries a moral argument. It is a testimony to courage, but more importantly it is a testimony to principles. Baba is prepared to risk his life to defend the honour of a young woman he barely knows. Although no explicit connection is made by the author, we are invited (implicitly) to compare Baba with Amir, who was not prepared to risk his personal safety to defend the honour of his closest friend.

The reappearance of Kamal is a variation on the same theme. He was not personally responsible for the rape of Hassan, but he allowed it to happen. Now he has had, in a sort of awful natural justice, the same thing done to him. His reaction is most significant: a sort of catatonic detachment, effectively a type of breakdown. It says a lot about the trauma that must have overcome Hassan, in similar circumstances. The act of rape – the ultimate enforcement of brutal domination – is also symbolic of the Russian invasion of Afghanistan. Kamal's death in the petrol tanker is a literal end, but he is already symbolically dead. In a brief but telling moment in which his grief stricken father, deprived now both of wife (killed by the Russians) and son, kills himself, somehow encapsulates the despair of many in the shattered, blood-stained country.

Chapter Eleven

America

The tensions of middle-eastern politics have been transplanted into the American-Afghan community, where Baba's unconventional and apparently pro-Israeli views arouse controversy. He 'loathes' President Jimmy Carter and as an admirer of 'hard man' Reagan is the 'lone Republican' in the apartment building. Baba still responds with physical violence when angry and overturns the magazine rack in the grocery store of an elderly Vietnamese couple because he resents being asked for ID when writing a cheque. Baba is working long hours in a gas station and Amir is a student. Amir is relieved to be '**someplace with no ghosts, no memories, and no sins**' and thus '**I embraced America**.'

Amir's graduation

When Amir graduates (from high school) Baba tells him '**I am *moftakhir* [proud], Amir.**' He takes Amir out for a celebration dinner. With typical largesse, Baba buys beer for the patrons of the bar and has soon 'started a party'. He buys Amir an old car, 'to go to college.' But just as Amir is enjoying the day, Baba adds, '**I wish Hassan had been with us today.**' Amir is being pressured by his father to study medicine, but

Quote

I didn't want to sacrifice myself for Baba anymore.
The last time I had done that, I had damned myself.

He decides to major in English and endeavours to convince his sceptical father that there is a possibility of making a living from writing.

Father and son start buying goods and selling at a flea market.

An entire section of the market is worked by expatriate Afghans and Baba. Baba introduces Amir to General Taheri, an acquaintance from Kabul and he meets Soraya, the general's beautiful daughter. Later Amir asks Baba about a 'story floating around' about Soraya. Baba gently teases Amir about his interest in Soraya and refers vaguely to a romantic relationship which 'didn't go well.' Amir thinks about Soraya as he lies in bed that night.

Amir meets Soraya

Commentary

Baba is no longer the politically and physically powerful man he once was but sometimes acts in the same autocratic and aggressive manner. Baba's treatment of the gentle, elderly Vietnamese couple is reprehensible and he is not entirely exonerated by Amir's explanation that he is 'still adjusting' to America. His pride in Amir's achievements is also reminiscent of the old Baba. The spontaneous celebration at the bar and his gift of a second-hand car are reminders of Amir's extravagant thirteenth birthday party. Yet here, as in the past, the celebrations are also about Baba, who becomes, as usual, the centre of attention. What is being celebrated is not only Amir's success. It is *Baba* who has produced a successful son and his capacity for grandiose hospitality is clearly a measure of his own success. Nevertheless, Baba has mellowed. Reduced circumstances, perhaps, and advancing years have rendered him a little more tolerant of his son's talent for 'making up stories.' The 'stories' circulated about Soraya are of a different kind and reveal deeply conservative attitudes to Afghan women which endure, despite the more tolerant culture of their adopted land.

Chapter Twelve

Amir counts the hours till he sees Soraya again, constantly finding excuses to visit her parents' marketstand. Baba notices Amir's interest in Soraya and cautions him. General Taheri is a proud Pashtun, he warns, who will defend the 'honour' and 'chastity' of his daughter. When Amir finds Soraya alone one day and speaks to her, asking her what she is reading, he feels 'the collective eyes of the flea-market Afghans' closely

Amir falls in love

observing them. Soraya's mother, Jamila, unexpectedly returns and is pleased that her daughter is attracting the attention of a young man. Amir becomes uneasily aware that he is in a position of power: '**I cringed a little at the position of power I'd been granted, and all because I had won at the genetic lottery that had determined my sex.**' For the next few weeks, Amir visits Soraya when she is alone and learns that she is studying to be a teacher. One day, her father returns suddenly and makes it clear that Amir's presence is unwelcome.

Baba's illness

Baba's 'cold' turns out to be something much more serious and while awaiting confirmation of the doctor's suspicion that it may be cancer, Amir prays to a God of whose existence he is unsure. He envies the 'faith and certainty' of the old mullah who taught him to pray. Terminal cancer is diagnosed and Baba obstinately refuses chemotherapy. Overcome with emotion, Amir feels his eyes 'welling up'. Yet he is also, as usual, thinking of himself, plaintively enquiring, 'what about me?' Baba sternly orders him to grow up and become a man.

The disease progresses rapidly and one day he has a terrifying seizure. Amir comforts him and spends the night sitting next to Baba's hospital bed. General Taheri and his wife and daughter visit Baba in the hospital. Soraya speaks tender words of comfort to Amir. Baba returns home and tells Amir to 'ask General Taheri for his daughter's hand'.

Amir and Soraya's betrothal

Baba phones General Taheri and organises a visit to discuss an '**honourable matter**'. Amir drives his father to the general's flat and returns home to await the telephone call. When it comes, Amir learns that Soraya's father has agreed to the marriage. Soraya then speaks to Amir, confessing that, as a rebellious eighteen-year old, she lived for a month with a drug-taking Afghan man. Soraya's strong sense of moral duty, allowing Amir the option of withdrawing his offer, is admirable and, although he admits to being 'bothered' by her loss of virginity, he reflects '**How could I, of all people, chastise someone for their past?**'

Commentary

Conservative Islamic attitudes to women are evident in General Taheri's protective attitude towards his daughter. Soraya's loss of virginity has almost completely destroyed her chances of a respectable marriage and the general is deeply suspicious of Amir's interest in her. His wife, Jamila, on the other hand, is delighted. Amir sees the 'barely veiled hope' in Jamila's eyes, and understands how 'a whisper here, and an insinuation there', sends prospective suitors fleeing 'like startled birds'. His comments on the power he has been granted by 'the genetic lottery', and his implicit condemnation of the sexual 'double standard' are gentle pointers to a more enlightened attitude towards women. Although 'bother[ed] a bit' by her confession, to his credit, Amir's moral qualms are not strong enough to override his love for Soraya. However, characteristically, Amir immediately thinks of himself, envying Soraya because *her* 'secret' is out. The festering wound of his betrayal of Hassan continues to eat away at Amir, just as surely as the carcinoma consumes Baba. Amir's enduring self-disgust, while undoubtedly painful, is much easier for him than openly admitting the truth, and he is no doubt quite right when he suspects that Soraya's courage is 'one of many ways' in which Soraya is 'a better person' than he is.

Chapter Thirteen

Amir and Soraya's marriage

The 'giving word' – a traditional Afghan engagement ceremony – takes place at Soraya's parents' house. The usual engagement period of a few months is dispensed with because of Baba's deteriorating health. The wedding, to which Baba contributes his life-savings of $35,000, takes place after 'frenzied preparations'. It is a solemn Islamic ceremony followed by traditional Afghan feasting. However, in the midst of his joy, Amir thinks: '**I remember wondering if Hassan too had married. And if so, whose face he had seen in the mirror under the veil?**'

After the banquet, Baba, Amir and Soraya return to Baba's apartment. Soraya suggests that they live with Baba so that she can help care for him, which she does with great devotion.

Baba's death

A month after the wedding, after a small family gathering, Baba drifts peacefully into a sleep from which he does not wake. His funeral at the mosque draws a large, respectful crowd. Amir notices the lines of cars pulling up, and groups of mourners, many of whom Amir barely knows, queue to shake his hand. The many people whom Baba has helped throughout his life express their gratitude to his son, and Amir realises,

Quote

How much of who I was, what I was, had been defined by Baba and the marks he had left on people's lives, My whole life, I had been "Baba's son". Now he was gone. Baba couldn't show me the way anymore; I'd have to find it on my own.

After the burial, Amir seeks out Soraya and finally gives way to his tears.

Amir gets to know the family

The general suffers from migraines and can be cantankerous and unreasonable. Amir rapidly becomes the object of Jamila's 'unblinking love', not only because she has found an audience for her 'impressive list of maladies' but also because he has saved her daughter from a dreadful fate: a 'husbandless' and 'childless' old age.

Soraya's past

At a cousin's wedding, Amir and Soraya overhear two middle-aged women discussing the bride's purity agreeing that the groom did well not to have married his cousin (Soraya). On the way home, Soraya breaks down, railing against a system that turns a blind eye to the sexual misconduct of men, but condemns women for the rest of their lives for 'one mistake'. She remembers her father arriving in Virginia with a gun, threatening to shoot her boyfriend and himself if Soraya did not come home. Amir again soberly reflects on his own past and finds it impossible to condemn Soraya. He acknowledges the **'double standard with which Afghan society sometimes treated [women]'**, and wonders if his father's 'liberal' views might account for his own more tolerant attitudes.

Soraya's career

Amir and Soraya move into their own apartment and General Taheri gives Amir a typewriter. Soraya enrols in a teaching course, much to her father's disapproval. He wants her to be a lawyer or a political scientist who will be able to play a future role in the reconstruction of Afghanistan. Soraya resents his interference and believes he just wants to boast about 'his attorney daughter' to his friends.

Amir completes his novel

Amir writes a 'father-son story' set in Kabul and contacts literary agencies. Eventually he receives a request for the manuscript and the novel is published the following year (1989). Amir and Soraya begin 'trying to have a child'. Amir wonders, '**What sort of father would I make ... I wanted to be just like Baba and I wanted to be nothing like him.**'

Infertility problems

After a year of failure, Amir and Soraya consult a doctor and undergo a series of tests. Amir 'passes' with 'flying colours'. Soraya is subjected to a battery of further tests, which prove inconclusive. The doctor finally suggests adoption, but for a variety of different reasons the family decides against it. Amir wonders if: '**perhaps something, someone, somewhere, had decided to deny me fatherhood for the things I had done. Maybe this was my punishment, and perhaps justly so.**' Amir uses the advance for his second novel as down payment on a house. As he lies in bed at night, he feels 'the emptiness in Soraya's womb' which 'sleeps between [them] like a newborn child'.

Commentary

Structurally located at the mid-point of the narrative, this important chapter marks Amir's crossing the boundary from childhood to adulthood. Three important milestones in his life take place in rapid succession: his marriage, his father's death and the publication of his novel. After a lifetime surrounded by men, Amir discovers the 'tenderness of a woman'. Soraya's tenderness also extends to her dying father-in law, and Baba, with the support of Soraya, finally reads some of Amir's writing. In doing so, he exhibits a new kind of paternal tenderness for a son with whom he has always been severe. Baba's death again exposes Amir's capacity for self-centredness, but also his insecurity about his ability to manage without the strength and guidance of the powerful man who had dominated his life.

Just as he had remembered Hassan on his wedding day, Amir also thinks of Hassan in connection with his childlessness, wondering whether it is divine retribution for his shameful past. Amir's assertion that he passed the fertility test 'with flying colours' subtly re-echoes the imagery of the kite contests and casts a shadow of 'failure' over Soraya; her 'empty womb' has denied him an opportunity to 'prove' his manhood by becoming a father. Metaphorically, however, Amir cannot truly 'be a man' until he demonstrates his moral courage and atones for the sins of his past.

Chapter Fourteen

Ten years have passed. As Amir lies in bed, he reflects somewhat bitterly on his childless marriage. Sometimes he thinks that love-making, while 'still good', is 'futile' (given their continuing child-lessness).

Rahim Khan's phone call

Amir's opportunity to atone for his past sins arrives in the form of a telephone call from Rahim Khan, ending in the words,

Quote

Come. There is a way to be good again.

Amir is shaken. He informs Soraya that he has to go to Pakistan, because Rahim is gravely ill. As he walks around Spreckels Lake, Amir sees a pair of kites and thinks about Rahim's words. He understands that Rahim knows about '**Assef, the kite, the money [and] the watch…**'

General Taheri falls and breaks his hip. His frailty and the 'passing of time' soften the relationship between Soraya and her father. Amir dreams of Hassan running through the snow, calling over his shoulder, 'for you, a thousand times over'. A week later, Amir boards a plane for Pakistan.

Commentary

Some readers may wish to question Amir's very traditional view of marriage and lovemaking as being primarily concerned with procreation. In conservative, patriarchal cultures, such attitudes remain unchallenged despite a broader cultural re-evaluation of the idea of 'family' in the late 20th and early 21st centuries. Amir's implicit adherence to these conservative cultural values, however, should not entirely overshadow the undoubted sadness of a couple unable to conceive.

The surprise phone call from Rahim Khan, and the hint in his strange challenge, are a pointer that we are about to move into the final phase of Amir's moral quest: his redemption. This is reinforced by the dream, in which he hears Hassan uttering those words of loyalty on the fateful day of the tournament. These words haunt Amir and underpin a moral duty to repay Hassan's loyalty.

Chapter Fifteen

The taxi driver in Peshawar describes the 'terrible' situation in Afghanistan. Amir tunes out, remembering the few months spent in Peshawar with Baba in 1981. He also remembers Rahim Khan's tearful farewell to Baba. Amir arrives at Rahim Khan's door to be greeted by 'a thing made of skin and bones pretending to be Rahim Khan.'

Amir's meeting with Rahim

Rahim Khan describes the situation in Afghanistan when it was under the control of the Northern Alliance between 1992 and 1996. The streets of Kabul were violent, with snipers and rockets being a constant danger. The Alliance destroyed, among other buildings, Baba's orphanage, killing many of the children. The Taliban, who 'kicked the Alliance out of Kabul', seemed like 'heroes'. In response to Amir's query about his health, Rahim tells Amir that he is dying. He also has a story to tell Amir about Hassan, with whom he had lived for a while in Baba's old house.

Commentary

Amir's desire to take Rahim Khan 'home' to find 'a good doctor' reveals a typically American 'optimism' in the possibility of scientific miracles, while Rahim's pragmatism underpins a characteristically eastern acceptance of 'God's will'. Rahim's quiet insistence on telling Amir about Hassan is his final duty to his oldest friend, Baba, and affords Amir an opportunity to 'be good again'. Even though Amir does not know whether such an opportunity is welcome, he cannot ignore the dying wishes of the man whose hand Amir's 'infant fingers' grasped so long ago. Rahim Khan is very well aware of this.

Chapter Sixteen

Rahim's story

Rahim tells his story (recounted in *his* words for this chapter). He was 'lonely', as most of his relatives had fled or been killed (after the Soviet invasion) so he went to Hazajarat (in 1986), to find Hassan. After a long search, he found him in a 'cluster of mud houses'. Hassan recognised Rahim instantly and took him inside to meet his pregnant wife, Farzana. Ali had been killed by a landmine – ironically, Hassan believed, because he had stepped on it with his crippled leg. Hassan had learned to read and write and asked Rahim to pass on a letter to Amir. Hassan wept when he heard of Baba's death.

Hassan and Farzana return to Kabul

Rahim talked Hassan and Farzana into returning with him to Baba's house in Kabul. Despite Rahim's protests, they moved into the humble hut of Hassan's childhood. He and Farzana cooked and tended the garden. Farzana gave birth to a stillborn baby girl but eventually, she conceived again.

Sanaubar's return

One day, during Farzana's pregnancy, a toothless, grey-haired old woman, clad in a burqa, arrived at the front gates. She collapsed. Her face had been badly cut, and she had not eaten for days. She asked for Hassan and revealed herself to be the mother who had deserted him in his infancy. Hassan and Farzarna nursed Sanaubar back to health and she delivered Hassan and Farzana's baby son: Sohrab. The child and his grandmother became insepara-ble. When Sanaubar died, Hassan was grief-stricken.

Just as his father had done, Sohrab became a talented kite runner and was equally deadly with the slingshot.

The Taliban take control

The rise of the Taliban caused Hassan grave concern. Rahim rejoiced because '**the war is over**', but Hassan's prophetic response was, '**God help the Hazaras.**' Two years later, the Taliban massacred the Hazaras in Maazar-i-Sharif.

Commentary

With this chapter, Amir (and the reader) are brought up-to-date with the mystery of Hassan. It is good news. The birth of his son and the return of his mother brought Hassan happiness, and it seems that only the return of Amir was needed to make his life complete.

With characteristic generosity of spirit, Hassan had only fond memories of the friend who betrayed him and drove him from his home. He lovingly cleaned Baba's old house as if he 'is preparing it for someone's return'.

Sanaubar's sudden return and her shockingly altered appear-ance suggest the difficulty of her life as a 'dishonourable' woman. She has clearly paid the price for a startling beauty which had 'tempted countless men into sin'. In a society where women have few rights and little freedom, Sanaubar's rebellious spirit and

Hazara status combined to make her a social outcast and the victim of shocking physical abuse. Her return to a traditional domestic role is crucial, in this society, to her moral salvation and she is able to die peacefully.

Yet, while the old man's story is a largely joyful one, there is still no explanation of why he has called Amir so urgently to him. We wait to see what other news is left unsaid.

Chapter Seventeen

Hassan's letter

In the envelope Rahim Khan hands him, Amir finds a photo of a man whose features he instantly recognises as those of his childhood companion. The accompanying letter, written in a childlike hand, recounts some of the terrors of daily life in Kabul under the Taliban. Women, in particular, are subjected to random acts of violence. Farzana suffered a brutal attack by a young Talib for raising her voice in the bazaar. Hassan has taught Sohrab to read and to use the slingshot with deadly accuracy. Hassan hopes that Amir will 'someday' return to Kabul, where he will find '**an old faithful friend waiting**'.

Hassan and Farzana shot

Six months after having written the letter, however, Hassan and Farzana were discovered by the Taliban to be living in Baba's house. They were ordered to leave and, when Hassan protested, he and Farzana were shot dead in the street. Rahim Khan asks Amir to go to Kabul and bring their orphaned son Sohrab back to Peshawar to be cared for by an American couple who run an orphanage.

Amir is reluctant to return to Kabul and offers to pay someone else to go. Rahim Khan responds angrily, accusing Amir of becoming what his father had predicted he might: '**a man who can't stand up to anything.**' Rahim pleads with Amir: '**What I'm asking from you is to grant an old man his dying wish.**'

Hassan's paternity

He then dramatically reveals that Ali had been sterile. He adds, in response to Amir's half asked question about who Hassan's real father was:

Quote

I think you know who.

Shocked and angered by the suggestion, Amir storms out of the apartment.

Commentary

Much is made of the brutality of the Taliban, the first of many such chapters on this subject. The despicable murder of Hassan and Farzana comes as a terrible shock, especially after the previous chapter, when things seemed so good for them. Rahim Khan's urgent mission now takes tangible form, and it is simultaneously Amir's greatest challenge: he needs to redeem himself by rescuing Hassan's son. Perhaps predictably, Amir tries to get out of this, even though his distress at the death of his childhood friend is genuine. The old Amir, still trying to find the easiest way, to avoid pain and danger, is very visible. He finds excuses not to return to Kabul and does not challenge Rahim Khan's accusation of cowardice. In one telling exchange he says,

Quote

You've always thought too highly of me, Rahim Khan.
And you've always been far too hard on yourself.

The shock announcement that Hassan was Baba's son startlingly reconfigures the central relationships of the novel. This is a deft move from the author, who raises the stakes for his protagonist.

Amir's reaction is understandable. His cruelty and treachery as a child is now revealed in its true context, and its fatal long term consequences (Hassan being left behind in Afghanistan, and eventually slaughtered by the Taliban) are even more devastating. He has inadvertently caused the death of his own brother, whose only sin was to love him. The moral argument of the novel – the need for Amir to make amends for his 'sins' – reaches this watershed moment at precisely the instant we have the most dramatic of all revelations. Amir's response will be the measure of his manhood.

Chapter Eighteen

Amir thinks about Baba and Hassan

Amir now recognises 'the signs' which should have alerted him to Baba's relationship with Hassan, most obviously his anger at Amir's attempt to get Hassan out of the house: '***Hassan's not going anywhere … He's staying right here with us, where he belongs. This is his home and we're his family.***' He bitterly resents the fact that Baba had lied for 'all those years' and considers his father to be (by his own definition) a '**thief,**' for stealing both of his sons' rights to the '**truth.**' Worse, Amir reflects that he and Baba are both sinners:

Quote

> Like father, like son ... As it turned out, Baba and I were more alike than I'd ever known. We had both betrayed the people who would have given their lives for us ... Rahim Khan had summoned me here to atone not just for my sins but for Baba's too.

Amir decides to go to Kabul

Amir realises that Baba has been right about one thing: that in order to grow up, he will need to start '**doing [his] own fighting.**' Rahim Khan welcomes Amir's decision and tells him that he will pray for him.

Commentary

Though one of the briefest chapters in the novel, it marks a key turning point. It is here that Amir finally faces up to his moral responsibilities. He faces his sins and the tragedy they have caused. He sees that he and his father share this moral weakness. For all his father's blustering ferocity and self-justification, he too has committed an unpardonable crime: siring a child by another man's wife and never publicly admitting it. His father is no longer the hero Amir thought. He too has a sin that must be redeemed.

In accepting that he must take up Rahim Khan's challenge, no matter how dangerous, and fighting his own battles, Amir moves from being a sympathetic but flawed character to a person who may earn the right to be admired. The complexity of the story makes his quest doubly important. For in redeeming himself, Amir will also redeem his father and metaphorically take his dead father's place as a 'hero.'

Chapter Nineteen

Amir's nationality challenged

Armed with Afghani money, traditional clothing and a false beard, Amir arrives in Afghanistan, feeling like 'a tourist in [his] own country.' Farid (the taxi driver organised by Rahim Khan) challenges Amir's right to call Afghanistan 'his' country, ' after twenty years of living in America.' Farid perceptively reminds him of the privileged and sheltered childhood he imagines Amir might have had. He then directs Amir's attention to an old man dressed in rags struggling to carry a large load of scrub grass – this, Farid claims is **'the real Afghanistan'**.

Amir a guest in Farid's house

In Jalalabad, Farid is warmly greeted by his brother, Wahid, and his family who, despite their poverty, make Amir welcome in their humble abode. Encouraged by their polite questions about his life in America, Amir begins to recount the plot of his first novel and is taken aback by a question about why he does not **'tell the rest of the world what the Taliban are doing [to Afghanistan]'**. When asked what has brought him back to Afghanistan, Amir briefly explains about Sohrab. He refers to Hassan, and this exchange takes place:

Quote

He was a friend of yours? ...
He was my half-brother.

Wahid replies, to Amir's embarrassment, **'You are an honourable man, Amir agha.'**

Amir is offered a meal

As Farid and Amir eat a simple meal, they are watched closely by Wahid's boys. Amir imagines that they are looking at his wristwatch, which he later gives to the youngest. The three boys soon lose interest. Farid offers to help Amir find Sohrab.

Amir's dream

As he sleeps on a straw mat on the floor, Amir's dream is filled with images of Hassan's death at the hands of the Taliban. With shocking clarity, Amir sees every grim detail and hears again the haunting words 'for you a thousand times over'. As the 'plume of smoke' swirls from the muzzle of the gun, the face of Hassan's executioner is revealed: ***'I am the man [who killed Hassan]'***.

Amir overhears conversation

Amir suddenly realises that, despite the wife's claim that they had already eaten, Wahid's family has gone hungry to feed their guests. Amir now understands that the object of the boys' interest while he was eating was not his watch but the food. Before he leaves, Amir plants 'a fistful of money' under a mattress.

Commentary

Evidence of Taliban control is everywhere; from the traditional attire that Amir is forced to wear to burqa-clad women to the fact that 'only the Taliban can afford meat'. Yet the stoicism and resilience of ordinary Afghans emerge in their regard for the importance of hospitality. Wahid reminds his wife that, 'we're hungry but we're not savages! He is a guest.' Honour, too, has survived the ravages of Taliban rule. Thus, Amir's parting gift must be concealed under a mattress, as Wahid's honour would be offended by the offer of payment for his generosity, despite the fact that his family is almost starving. Amir's misunderstanding of the boys' interest as he eats, and the ridiculously inappropriate gift of a useless western trinket 'which tells the time in any city in the world', reveal how far he still is from understanding 'the real Afghanistan'.

Amir's troubled dream is a graphic representation of his enduring sense of guilt. Amir's 'vision' of Hassan 'kneeling on the street' with 'blood' on his pants merges the horrifying images of the child as he was raped, and the adult as he awaited death. In both instances it is Hassan's unswerving loyalty to Amir that is the instrument of his undoing. Amir's vision of his *own* face behind the smoking muzzle of the executioner's gun reveals his awareness of this, and heightens his belated sense of responsibility to his dead friend. Although a seemingly simple exchange, the open admission of his blood relationship with Hassan is the first time Amir has spoken of the bond that ties them – which has now become the major motivation for his actions and the focal point of his moral quest.

Chapter Twenty

Amir arrives in Kabul

Amir is shocked by the devastation of the villages as they draw closer to Kabul. In squalid, rubble-filled streets, beggars, mostly women and children, squat miserably at every corner. Ominously, there are virtually no men to be seen. As they drive through the ravaged streets nostalgically recreating the old Kabul, a 'beard-patrol' vehicle approaches. One of its occupants fixes Amir with a menacing gaze. Farid warns Amir 'never' to stare at the Taliban.

Amir learns about his mother

Amir gives money to a filthy old beggar from whom they ask directions to the new orphanage. The beggar informs Amir that he was formerly a respected university lecturer and coincidentally, it emerges, a colleague of Amir's mother. Dr Rasul, as he was formerly known, fondly remembers the beautiful Sofia Akrami. Amir learns more about his mother from the old man than he 'ever did from Baba'.

The orphanage

At the orphanage, Amir produces the photograph of Hassan and Sohrab, only to be told by the man who opens the orphanage door that he has never seen the child. Amir persists, desperately seeking to reassure the man that they mean Sohrab no harm. When Amir also mentions Sohrab's skill with the slingshot, the door is opened again. The man introduces himself as Zaman, the director of the orphanage.

Zaman takes Amir and Farid through the orphanage, recounting the tragic stories of the children who live in the appalling conditions there – whom Zaman describes as '**the lucky ones**'. He then informs Amir that it may be 'too late' to save Sohrab. Zaman explains that a 'Talib official' comes 'every month or two' to 'take' a child away, 'usually a girl'. Farid is so enraged that he tries to strangle Zaman. Zaman reveals that Sohrab was taken a month ago. He tells Amir and Farid that if they go the Ghazi stadium the following day, they will see the Talib official, who will appear at half-time 'wearing black sun-glasses'.

Sohrab's situation

Commentary

The portrait of Taliban-controlled Kabul is devastating. Not only is the city a wasteland, where even university lecturers have been reduced to beggars, but the Taliban themselves are portrayed as brutally violent and corrupt, abusing their power for personal gain. The orphanage is an appropriate symbol of their ruthless regime. Desperate mothers, forbidden to work and with no husband to support them, bring their starving children daily to Zaman's door, only to be turned away because the orphanage is 'filled beyond capacity'. The 'lucky ones', whose parents are both dead, often fall victim to the perverted whims of a Taliban official. Things are so bad that Zaman is forced to accept the 'filthy money' he receives as 'payment' for a child, in order to buy food for the others and prevent them starving. The implied rape of innocent children recalls the earlier rape of Hassan by the thug, Assef. There is no need for Hosseini to comment. His message is shockingly clear.

Chapter Twenty-One

Amir visits his childhood home

Farid takes Amir to the Wazir Akbar Khan district, where the 'important people' live: **'The people behind the Taliban. The real brains of this government, if you can call it that: Arabs, Chechens, Pakistanis ... [the] guests.'**

Amir recognises Baba's house. As he looks he is filled with painful memories. Farid advises, '**Nothing that you remember has survived. Best to forget**' to which Amir replies '**I don't want to forget anymore.**' Amir climbs the hill to discover that the old pomegranate tree is now 'wilted and leafless'. Later that night, after sharing a pleasant meal and swapping a few jokes, Farid asks Amir why he is 'really' in Afghanistan. When told, he exclaims, contemptuously, '**You came all the way from America for ... a Shi'a?**'

Execution at Ghazi stadium

Thousands of people fill the stadium for the afternoon's entertainment, which will include a soccer match and a public execution. At half time, a couple who have 'dishonour[ed] the sanctity of marriage' are driven onto the field. A Talib official wearing black sunglasses appears and stones the couple to death. Their 'bloodied corpses' are 'unceremoniously tossed' into the back of pick-up trucks. Amir cannot watch. Farid whispers, '**And they call themselves Muslims.**' The soccer match continues and Farid manages to arrange a meeting with 'the man in white'.

Commentary

Despite Farid being a supportive ally, his own deeply ingrained racism comes out in the comment about Amir's commitment to a Shi'a (the other race, and sect of Islam). Amir's shock leads him to think that maybe Afghanistan is, after all, 'a hopeless place' because of this ancestral intolerance, if not hatred. Farid's attitude and the Taliban impulse for 'ethnic cleansing' arise from the same racist sentiments which Amir himself had once endorsed as he watched Assef rape Hassan.

The afternoon at the Ghazi stadium provides another, if far more disturbing, example of intolerance. It is a striking way of making a point about the horrors of totalitarian states, and any kind of extremism. Again, as with the rape of Hassan, Amir cannot watch. Yet the few details described are horrifying. The power of the scene is captured through the sounds of the woman's screams, the gasping of the crowd and the dreadful image of the bloodied corpses.

There are echoes in the scene of the Colosseum in ancient Rome. There is mockery of the fat cleric who intones coldly over the condemned pair. Above all there is the chilling figure of the man in sunglasses, whose messianic pretensions (in a 'sparkling white garment' he faces the crowd – his arms 'spread like those of Jesus on the cross') and sadism are all too plain.

Yet even under the noses of the Taliban enforcers, people still defy the absurdly rigid moral code, as the 'scrawny boy' selling 'very sexy' photographs demonstrates. Clearly driven by hunger, the child is forced to risk a brutal 'flogging' in order to survive. The existence of these photographs suggests that there is a ready market for them, which also indicates a subversive resistance to Taliban control. And given the decadent inclinations of the man in the black sunglasses (indicated by his buying a boy for sex), the higher ranking Taliban officials exempt themselves from the strict moral code they so brutally enforce on others.

Chapter Twenty-Two

Amir meets 'the Talib'

Farid drives Amir to his appointment and waits in the car. Amir is frisked and shown into a room to await the arrival of the man in white – the man who had taken Sohrab from the orphanage. Amir, hardly believing his temerity, feels 'utterly alone' as he contemplates the 'insanity' of what he is doing. The tall Talib enters, accompanied by two armed men. In response to Amir's traditional Islamic greeting, the Talib rips Amir's false beard from his face and laughs. He muses on the benefits of public execution which he describes euphemistically as 'public justice'. He also enthusiastically recounts the joys of 'liberation' describing an orgy of shooting men and boys (the massacre of Mazar) 'in front of their families' as doing 'God's work'.

Amir switches the conversation to the topic of Sohrab, and the Talib responds by threatening to have Amir arrested and charged with treason for deserting his country. Suddenly he enquires if Amir would like to see '[his] boy'. Sohrab is sum-

Amir dicovers 'the Talib's' identity

moned and Amir is overwhelmed by his resemblance to his father. Sohrab's eyes are 'darkened with mascara' and his cheeks coloured with rouge. Sohrab is ordered to dance, and when the music stops he is summoned to the Talib's side. The two guards are ordered to leave the room and the Talib slides his hand 'up and down the boy's belly'. Suddenly the Talib wonders aloud **'Whatever happened to the old *Babalu*?'** Amir is shocked to realise that the Talib is none other than the sadistic bully, Assef.

Assef's story

Assef and his parents had been arrested by the Communists in 1980 and while in jail, he was beaten by a sadistic commandant. The beatings dislodged Assef's painful kidney stones, which he interpreted as a 'message from God' that he was meant to live 'for a reason'.

Quote

I've been on a mission since.
What mission is that? ... Stoning adulterers? Raping children? Flogging women for wearing high heels? Massacring Hazzaras? All in the name of Islam?

Assef replies that '**Afghanistan is like a beautiful mansion littered with garbage, and someone has to take out the garbage,**' to which Amir replies '**In the west .... They call it ethnic cleansing.**'

Amir reiterates his desire to take Sohrab. Unexpectedly Assef tells Amir to 'take him', but as Amir and Sohrab are leaving, Assef mentions some 'unfinished business'. He calls the guards back in, instructing them not to interfere and then dismisses them. Assef takes his brass knuckles from his pocket and challenges Amir to a fight.

Assef and Amir fight

The bloody fight is recounted as a series of images and memories. Amir remembers Assef's brass knuckles 'flashing in the afternoon light ... blood from [his] split upper lip staining the mauve carpet ... Sohrab screaming ...the knuckles shattering [his] jaw... a snapping sound under his left eye ... Yet he also remembers laughing.

Quote

What was so funny was that, for the first time since the winter of 1975, I felt at peace ... My body was broken ... but I felt *healed.* Healed at last.

As Assef prepares to land another (possibly fatal) blow, Sohrab loads his slingshot with a brass ball and fires at Assef, dislodging his eye. Writhing in agony, Assef screams at them to 'get out' and they hurriedly make their escape.

Commentary

The re-appearance of Assef is a master stroke, well concealed in the narrative and delivering considerable dramatic impact at what is already a point of high anxiety in the narrative. What is clever in Hosseini's management of this character is how, at a moment when the murderous insanity of the Taliban is already painfully clear, he makes their representative a character already (and long since) established as a monster.

Assef, the arch-villain, is associated with Hitler (through his gift for Amir's thirteenth birthday and his open admiration of the German dictator). Thus, the Taliban's ethnic cleansing is implicitly connected with Hitler's genocide. Assef is also, as most bullies are, a coward, who needs the support of brainless henchmen and brass knuckles to exert his power. The other indication of Assef's evil nature is his paedophilia – symbolising the annihilation of purity and innocence. What is not made entirely clear is whether Assef's sexuality is also (in Hosseini's mind) an indication of moral corruption. Assef's character is a devastating comment on Taliban officialdom, their hypocrisy, their savagery, their unholy 'mission', which is nothing more than thuggery hiding behind religion.

We must ask perhaps how we feel about the ending of this climactic chapter. Hosseini's own hint that it is 'justice' – insofar as the boy unwittingly fulfils the threat made by his father many years ago – is clear enough. It *does* raise the rather difficult problem of whether violence *is* a necessary response to (and perhaps the only cure for) evil. This theme will be played out explicitly in the next chapter.

Chapter Twenty-Three

Amir treated in hospital

Amir lapses in and out of consciousness but gradually realises the extent of his considerable injuries and that he is 'lucky to be alive'. The most significant of his injuries is to his upper lip: **'The impact had cut your upper lip in two ... clean**

down the middle ... Like a harelip.'

Amir attempts to talk to Sohrab

Farid and Sohrab come to visit and Sohrab finds that he is '**the Amir agah [his] father told [him] about.**' When Farid asks what happened, Amir replies '**Let's just say we both got what we deserved.**' Amir thanks Sohrab for saving his life. In response to Amir's query about Rahim Khan, Farid informs him that he has disappeared but has left a letter for Amir.

Rahim Khan's letter

When Farid picks Sohrab up later that night, Amir reads Rahim Khan's letter. Rahim apologises for his silence over Baba's infidelity and acknowledges Amir and Hassan's 'right to know.' He describes Amir as a 'troubled little boy,' but points out the positive side of his pain: '**A man who has no conscience, no goodness, does not suffer.**' He also explains that Baba was so 'hard' on Amir because he could not openly acknowledge his love for Hassan, so he took it out on Amir, 'the socially legitimate' son .

Quote

You are still angry and I realise it is far too early to expect you to accept this, but maybe someday you will see that when your father was hard on you, he was also being hard on himself. Your father, like you, was a tortured soul ...

Rahim says that redemption is what his father wanted. '**And that, I believe, is what true redemption is, Amir jan, when guilt leads to good.**' He concludes by begging Amir not to look for him.

Farid agrees to seek out the Caldwells – the owners of the orphanage mentioned by Rahim Khan. As Amir and Sohrab play cards, they talk about Hassan, who had told Sohrab that Amir was 'the best friend he ever had.' Amir asks Sohrab to be *his* friend.

Amir must leave Afghanistan

The next day Amir decides to leave the hospital, despite his pain. He is fearful of the Taliban finding out where they are. He plans to fly home in a few days, but Farid's news that the Caldwells do not exist changes his plans.

Sohrab goes to Islamabad

Sohrab cannot remain on his own in Peshawar and Farid cannot take him into his family. During the four hour ride to Islamabad, Amir remembers the blood on the seat of Hassan's pants after he was raped. He remembers Rahim Khan's words: there is 'a way to be good again.'

Commentary

Past and present converge quite dramatically in this and the preceding chapter. As Amir dreams of Baba wrestling the black bear, he 'becomes' his father: 'He's *me.* I am wrestling the bear.' In wrestling with and overcoming his shameful past Amir has finally become an adult, symbolically replacing his dead father and atoning for his father's sins. In another echo of the past, Sohrab saves Amir, just as his father once had, but while Hassan's threat had sufficed to subdue Assef, Sohrab's deadly aim does indeed change the bully's name to 'one-eyed Assef'. Amir and Sohrab play cards, just as Amir and Hassan had, and Amir observes that Sohrab *was* Hassan. Both sons 'become' their fathers, finally giving expression to the unspoken love of Baba for Hassan.

A striking piece of symbolism is the split lip. This pointedly connects Amir and Hassan, making them (symbolically) physically similar, and expressing their belated connectedness as brothers. It also makes a point about suffering. Hassan suffered for Amir and the blood on his pants was the sign. Now Amir suffers for Hassan, and the multiple injuries, the blood and his split lip are the signs.

However, there is something else. An unsettling parallel between Assef and Amir is hinted at in Amir's dream where Assef tells him that although he (Amir) had nursed with Hassan, it is Assef who is his 'twin'. Amir understands that while Assef had brutally raped Hassan, it was Amir who had betrayed him, which was worse. Amir's acknowledgement of this is essential. Amir's awareness of this debt of guilt, made even more explicit in Rahim Khan's letter, informs the unresolved 'question' of what to do with Sohrab. It is clear that Sohrab (through Amir) can find 'a way to be good again.'

Chapter Twenty-Four

Amir is grateful for Farid's help and pays him generously. More importantly, friendship and mutual respect has developed between the two men.

Sohrab appears to be asleep when Amir returns to the hotel

Amir farewells Farid

room after farewelling Farid so he takes some painkillers and goes to sleep. When he awakes, Sohrab is gone. After a frantic search, Amir realises that he must have gone to the mosque he had taken such an interest in on the way into Islamabad. Indeed he finds Sohrab sitting near the mosque.

Sohrab's guilt

Sohrab talks of Hassan; he admits that he is starting to 'forget' the faces of his parents and Amir gives him the polaroid snapshot. Sohrab then asks tearfully, **'Will God punish me in hell for what I did to that man?'** He adds, **'Father used to say it's wrong to hurt even bad people. Because they don't know any better, and because bad people sometimes become good**.' Amir reassures him, saying,

Quote

That there are bad people in this world, and sometimes bad people stay bad. Sometimes you have to stand up to them. What you did to that man is what I should have done to him all those years ago. You gave him what he deserved, and he deserved even more.

Amir assures Sohrab that he is not 'dirty and full of sin'. He reaches out for Sohrab who, at last, allows himself to be comforted. Amir asks Sohrab if he would like to come and live in America.

Amir tells Sohrab that he and Hassan were brothers

As Amir and Sohrab picnic in the park, Amir tells Sohrab that **'Your father and I were brothers,'** and adds, in answer to Sohrab's question about Baba, **'I think he loved us equally but differently**.' He explains that Hassan never knew and that he only recently discovered the truth. Sohrab enquires whether this is 'because he was a Hazara,' and Amir acknowledges that it was. Amir asks Sohrab if he has thought about living in America, and Sohrab admits to being scared, but tells Amir that he never wants to 'go to another orphanage.' Amir promises that it will never happen.

Amir phones Soraya

Amir has been away for almost a month before he contacts Soraya, who has been 'sick' with worry. He tells her that he is 'bringing a little boy home' whom he would like them to adopt. Then he tells her 'everything'. By the time he has finished his story, she is 'weeping', but assures Amir that if Sohrab is his family, he is her family too.

The consular official, Raymond Andrews, appears uninterested in Amir and Sohrab but asks to hear their story. Amir gives

The American Embassy

him the barest details, and Andrews asks if anyone 'can attest' to the fact that Amir is Sohrab's 'half-uncle'. He insists that official documentation is required to prove that Amir is an orphan. Andrews advises Amir to 'give up' the idea of taking Sohrab to America, as there are 'significant obstacles' to be overcome. Amir calls Soraya again; she is excited at the prospect of Sohrab's arrival, and has asked an Afghan friend in with 'INS buddies' to help with Sohrab's application. Sohrab has become withdrawn again since the interview with Raymond Andrews.

Amir enlists the help of Omar Faisal

Omar Faisal, a lawyer experienced in such cases, arrives. After listening to the 'un-censored version' of Amir's story, he admits that it will be a 'tough battle' and one which Amir is 'not likely' to win. Amir's 'options' are limited and unpalatable: living with Sohrab in Pakistan for two years and then seeking asylum on his behalf, or 'relinquishing' Sohrab to an orphanage in Pakistan and going through the lengthy process of applying for adoption. Amir explains to Sohrab that he might have to 'wait' for a little while, and that he might need to 'stay in a home for kids'. Sohrab is terrified and begs Amir to 'promise' that he will not send him to an orphanage.

Later that night, Soraya calls with good news: a humanitarian visa might be arranged which will get Sohrab into America. Amir goes to tell Sohrab the 'great news', only to find him unconscious in the bathtub with his wrists slashed.

Commentary

This chapter again tackles the difficult question of violence and revenge (in the words of the Old Testament, 'an eye for an eye, a tooth for a tooth'). Interestingly, it is the child who offers the standard pacifist argument, which significantly he has learnt from his father, the virtuous Hassan. The child's 'argument' is a telling one. That Amir is able to rebut it with an argument based on reprisal and 'justice' does not necessarily end the matter – or indicate that Hosseini endorses Amir's view. Such arguments can sound perilously like the mad arguments of the Taliban.

In another sense, of course, Amir is right to reassure Sohrab that he has not sinned and will not be punished. There was an element of self-defence in the act which saved Amir (and Sohrab). It is also proper to try and comfort a traumatised little boy. The scene by the mosque is a warm one, as Amir tries to get Sohrab to trust him and, in time, to love him, as he has begun to love Sohrab. Telling Sohrab about their 'blood' relationship and his debt of gratitude to Hassan is a tentative step in the direction of mutual trust. Unfortunately, Amir's rash 'promise' not to allow Sohrab 'ever' to return to an orphanage is another step, one that while well intentioned, is rapidly shown to be somewhat reckless.

Amir immediately encounters the 'insanity' of western bureaucracy, ironically juxtaposed with the insanity of the Taliban regime, where 'the rules', however brutal or ridiculous, are enforced with no regard for compassion or commonsense. Amir's allusion to Victor Hugo's novel, *Les Miserables* (with the characters Jean Valjean, the criminal/hero, and Javert, the policeman/villain) reinforces the image of an inhumane and obsessive bureaucracy. Amir, again making errors, has to do an about face on the orphanage issue, and Sohrab, who is beginning to trust Amir, withdraws. We are not to know as this chapter ends if Sohrab has become another victim of Amir's indiscretions. The blood is literal enough, but also symbolic (again). The child's suicide attempt reveals his complete loss of faith in the honesty and reliability of adults.

Chapter Twenty-Five

Amir visits Sohrab

Waiting at the hospital, Amir throws a makeshift prayer rug on the floor and utters the few words of prayer that he can remember. '**I see now that Baba was wrong, there is a God, there always has been … there has to be.**' He prays that his '**sins have not caught up with him**' again. '**My hands are stained with Hassan's blood; I pray God doesn't let them get stained with the blood of his boy too.**' After several tense hours, having heard nothing, Amir feels a tap on the shoulder and a doctor informs him, '**He is alive.**'

After three days in the ICU, Sohrab is transferred to a ward. Amir visits him but Sohrab will not speak. Amir tortures himself with regret about falling asleep when he was so vulnerable. When the child eventually does speak, it is to say plaintively '**I want my old life back,**' and to tell Amir that he wishes he had been left 'in the water' to die. Amir begs his forgiveness. This is the last time for 'almost a year' that Amir hears Sohrab speak.

Finally, Sohrab neither declines nor accepts Amir's 'offer' and

Sohrab arrives in America

Amir brings Hassan's son from 'the certainty of turmoil' in Afghanistan to the 'turmoil of uncertainty' in America. Soraya picks them up at the airport and Amir has a glimpse of the 'mother she might have been.' Sohrab does not respond in any way. At home with Amir and Soraya, he passively accepts whatever is offered but remains silent. That night, Amir finds the polaroid photo under Sohrab's pillow.

Sohrab meets Soraya's parents

General Taheri and his wife come for dinner and are alarmed at Amir's injuries which he tells them are the result of a mugging. During dinner and after some general conversation about Afghanistan, the general finally asks **'why there is a Hazara boy living with [his] daughter.'** Amir explains, somewhat tersely, that Sohrab is Baba's grandson. He also informs the general that 'never again,' in Amir's presence, will he refer to Sohrab as 'Hazara boy.'

A difficult year follows in which Sohrab's continued silence casts a shadow over the lives of Amir and Soraya. The twin towers are destroyed (2001) and America bombs Afghanistan (2002).

The gathering in Fremont

Early the following year, Sohrab accompanies the family to a gathering of Afghans at a park in Fremont. There is traditional Afghan music and food and friendly chatter but Sohrab, as usual, is silent and detached. During the afternoon, Soraya draws Amir's attention to half-a-dozen kites fluttering in the sky. Amir buys a kite from a vendor and shows it to Sohrab. Amir talks about Hassan and his skill as a kite runner. He asks Sohrab to help him fly the kite but, receiving no response, runs 'solo'. He is transported (mentally) back to the peak moment of his childhood. Suddenly he feels 'a presence' next to him. Sohrab has followed him. Amir holds out the kite and Sohrab hesitantly '[takes] the string.'

A green kite closes in and Sohrab hands the string back to Amir and takes the spool. The 'vacant' look in his eyes disappears as he and Amir battle the green kite. Before long, the green kite is downed and onlookers are cheering. Amir sees **'A smile.'** Amir offers to 'run the kite' and when Sohrab nods, Amir hears himself repeat Hassan's words: **'For you, a thousand times over.'**

Commentary

Having repaid his debt to Hassan by rescuing his son, and being instrumental in punishing his persecutor, Amir might expect to be at peace with himself. Yet life is not so simple, as Amir realises. His foolishness in abandoning the boy emotionally in his hour of need, and the disastrous result, are another blood debt he owes. As well as begging forgiveness, literally, of the child, he turns to God. This is an important and surprising development. Just as Baba was a secular man, who actively distrusted the mullahs, Amir has thus far been a sceptic too. The sudden need for God however is understandable given the grief he is experiencing. The 'conversion' speaks volumes about his change of heart, and suffering – and that is the real point.

It is also interesting that Hosseini has his protagonist become a devout Muslim. In the light of the undeniable anti-Taliban, and anti-mullah, strains in the novel, this is a development worth commenting on. The author seems to be making the point that religion itself is an understandable crutch in time of need, perhaps even a deep yearning for meaning and comfort that must be fulfilled. Amir's rejuvenated religious faith is also a reconnection with his historical past: an affirmation of his Islamic heritage. In a western, post-September 11 world, Islamic culture has often been misunderstood. Amir's celebration of Islam in Hosseini's semi-autobiographical novel affirms the traditions and the spiritual foundations of an ancient culture, while still condemning the lunatic zealotry (specifically the excesses of the Taliban) that are sometimes confused with the religion.

The kite battle in the park finally (and perhaps a trifle too neatly) lays to rest the demons of the past and provides, in Sohrab's almost imperceptible smile, a glimmer of hope for the future. Amir's final words, 'I ran', reverberate with echoes of his childhood betrayal. Faced with the choice of standing up for Hassan in the alley all those years ago, or running, Amir's words were also 'I ran.' This time, however, Amir is not running *away*. As he re-enacts the role of Hassan, he finally repays the loyalty of his childhood friend, and his reward is the small indication that Sohrab *will* slowly be rehabilitated after all.

It is a quietly joyful ending and a welcome relief from the suffering. Above all, it is a resolution of the moral argument which has dominated the text. Given genuine contrition, and acts of compassion and kindness to make amends – not to mention the pain that goes with them – Amir *does* indeed find redemption at last. He has become 'good again.' His running for Sohrab is symbolically an act of humbling himself before Hassan, and this is the posthumous cancellation of that debt.

Notes on Characters

Amir

Quote

… my entire life … had been a cycle of lies, betrayals and secrets.

Cannot meet father's expectations

Amir is an insecure child, desperate to win the affection of a powerful and successful father. He is physically 'inadequate': prone to carsickness, unable to excel at sport and incapable of fighting his own battles. Burdened by his overwhelming sense of inadequacy and desperate to win his father's affection, Amir 'sacrifices' Hassan, thinking only of his triumphant return with the blue kite, the 'smile on [his] father's lips' and the warmth of his embrace. This enables him to 'forget' what he has done, and reveals the depth of his longing for affection and acceptance.

Friend and brother

Friendship and brotherhood converge in the relationship between Amir and Hassan. While the two boys have fed from the same breast and are inseparable childhood companions, Amir always thinks of Hassan as his 'servant'. Amir often mocks or patronises his faithful Hazara friend, whom he betrays and cruelly rejects. It is Hassan who exemplifies true friendship in this relationship, living out the words: 'for you, a thousand times over.' Brotherhood, however, has always been more complex. The ancient story of Cain and Abel, the sons of Adam and Eve, provides an iconic story of 'sibling rivalry'. In that narrative, which appears both in the Bible *and* the Koran, Cain is envious of his brother Abel, and one day kills him. God's question regarding the whereabouts of Abel elicits Cain's celebrated rhetorical answer 'Am I my brother's keeper?' Cain is cursed to wander the Earth, a terrible punishment indeed but Amir's is perhaps worse – he is tormented by years of shame and regret. It is only when he finally affirms the bonds of brotherhood, that Amir proves himself to be a worthy friend and a morally responsible human being.

Mature adult

The traditional milestones of adolescence, graduation, marriage and career mark Amir's rite of passage from child to adult. Yet he has a more dangerous and difficult rite of passage to endure if he is to become a mature adult. As a child, Amir is often self-centred, cowardly and treacherous. The adult Amir must overcome his weaknesses and atone for the 'sins' of his past. Amir must also take the place of his father. Baba's death leaves a gap that Amir is psychologically and morally unqualified to fill *until he has redeemed himself.* Amir's 'maturity' is finally achieved through his relationship with Sohrab, from whom Amir learns about paternal responsibility.

Amir as a hero

In the traditional 'quest narrative', the (male) hero must prove his worthiness by confronting danger. In doing so, he overcomes evil, conquers his own fears and failings and ultimately reaffirms his society's moral values. In this respect, Amir certainly fulfils the traditional role of the 'hero'. The values he affirms are the importance of family, respect for human life and dignity, the principles of justice and honour, the need for freedom and the importance of spiritual faith.

Yet Amir is a very flawed hero and it is often difficult to admire, or even to like him. Indeed he often does not like himself. Nevertheless, he redeems himself and is 'rewarded' by the (implied) fulfilment of his dream of fatherhood. Whether or not he *is* a 'hero', however, is a question worthy of careful consideration.

Hassan

Quote

For you, a thousand times over.

Loyal friend

Hassan exemplifies unwavering loyalty and generosity of spirit. Disregarding his own fear, Hassan courageously defends Amir against Assef and remains loyal, even after being betrayed. Hassan willingly sacrifices himself, supporting Amir's lie by admitting to 'stealing' the watch and the money. He tells his son that Amir was the 'best friend' he ever had, and dies defending the home to which Amir might one day return. Hassan's physical disability endows him (for most of his childhood) with a 'permanent smile'; a symbol of his uncomplaining acceptance of his lot in life.

Victimised Hazara

Hassan stoically accepts his inferior social status; after years of vilification and victimisation, the Hazaras' 'inferiority' is taken for granted. Thus Assef feels justified in raping Hassan, as he is 'only a Hazara' (although Assef could undoubtedly 'justify' any moral outrage, as indeed he later does). More shockingly, Amir justifies his cowardice the same way. Yet Hassan displays more courage than his Pashtun 'friend' and is clearly Amir's intellectual equal. He also has sufficient self-respect to 'challenge' Amir's 'dirt-eating' test of loyalty. Through his servitude to Amir and his violation by Assef, Hassan represents his suffering people, and perhaps by implication, persecuted minorities everywhere. Hosseini's sympathetic portrayal of the harelipped Hazara is an implicit condemnation of all kinds of racial prejudice.

It is certainly worth considering whether Hassan is a hero. Certainly he is the moral touchstone or centre of the novel. His virtues – love, compassion, honesty, patience, humility, courage, even wisdom itself – are very clearly what the author implicitly argues should be the goals of everyone.

Baba

Quote

There is only one sin, only one. And that is theft. Every other sin is a variation of theft.

Power and success

Described by Amir as 'a force of nature,' Baba is a complex character. Outwardly he is the epitome of masculinity: physically strong, successful in business, charismatic and sexually attractive. Like Amir, Baba is also the son of a successful father, a 'highly-regarded judge', in whose footsteps Baba does not follow. To prove himself his father's equal, Baba takes delight in achieving the impossible, from marrying a 'princess' to building an orphanage. He must also display his wealth and power by building the 'most beautiful house' in the district and entertaining lavishly. Beneath the impressive façade, however, is his carefully concealed emptiness and insecurity.

Baba's darker side

Baba's disappointment in his son is a further indication of his insecurity. His inability to accept a child who is so unlike him indicates Baba's need for affirmation. Ironically, like his son, Baba too has a guilty secret. Either lust or loneliness draws Baba to the bed of Sanaubar, 'the wife of his servant.' But Ali is also his friend and Baba dishonours him 'in the single worst way an Afghan man can be dishonoured.' While Baba is a courageous man, willing to fight against injustice and dishonour, he is also sometimes violent and unreasonable. Only Rahim Khan ever 'dares' to criticise him. Consequently, with no capacity for self-reflection, Baba shuts himself off from his feelings and he must constantly surround himself with people to fill the emotional void in his life.

Baba mellows with age

As political changes destabilise Afghanistan, Baba realises that it is not a good place for Amir. He sacrifices his own happiness for his son's future, immigrating to America and taking on a menial job to support Amir's education. There is, as Amir belatedly realises, an element of self-punishment in this humiliation. Finally, Baba is proud of Amir's academic success. He finally accepts Amir's 'difference' and reads his journal. However, he must conceal his paternal pride, just as he had concealed his grief over the death of his wife; for tenderness is perceived as weakness. Baba rapidly declines. The cancer consuming him symbolises his loss of power and provokes a characteristically defiant resistance. Baba's funeral is a fitting tribute to a powerful man whose intimidating façade had concealed a warm heart and quiet generosity that made a difference in many lives.

Sohrab

Quote

I want my old life back.

Innocent victim

Sohrab is the innocent victim of an unstable and corrupt adult world. Brutally orphaned by the Taliban, Sohrab falls into the hands of Assef, his father's childhood tormentor and rapist. Sohrab becomes the sexual plaything of a perverted maniac who strips him of his dignity, making him feel 'dirty' and 'sinful'. Like his father, Sohrab is intrinsically good, and is still able to wonder if bad people 'sometimes become good.' He has also inherited his father's skill and courage, eventually blinding Assef in one eye as his father had once threatened to do.

Dreadfully damaged by his horrific experiences, Sohrab resists Amir's initial attempts to win his trust. Although he begins to come out of himself in response to the gentle overtures of his uncle Amir, his greatest fear is then rekindled when Amir goes back on his promise. Sohrab's suicide attempt reveals the depths of his despair in the face of another 'betrayal'. Sohrab's long silence is a barrier against further pain – if he closes himself down he cannot be hurt.

Hope for the future

The symbol of the soaring kite is an appropriate one for the beginning of Sohrab's slow healing. The kite becomes a bridging symbol for both the old life and the new and draws a line of 'kinship' between Amir, Sohrab and Hassan. Sohrab's faint smile as he and Amir vanquish the 'green kite' implies that there is hope for recovery and even, perhaps, trust.

Soraya

Quote

I make one mistake and suddenly everyone is talking ... and I have to have my face rubbed in it for the rest of my life.

Independent and defiant

Intelligent, spirited and sensitive, Soraya is nevertheless relatively marginal. She is defined (like the other women in the text) as a daughter and/or a wife, and in this regard, reflects the values of patriarchal society. Soraya's choice of reading material, *Wuthering Heights*, is significant. Emily Bronte's novel about a passionate young woman, who defies patriarchal authority for the sake of love, has a particular resonance for Soraya who, like Bronte's heroine, is also independent and defiant. Like the character in the novel, Soraya also pays a heavy price for her rebellion.

Soraya maintains her independent attitude. She stands up to her father, achieves academic success and makes her own career choice. However, her role is primarily domestic and her career is always secondary to her husband's. Soraya's support of Amir's literary aspirations and of his relationship with Sohrab is unequivocal, and it is integral to Amir's success.

Soraya's role as wife

It is worth pausing to reflect on Amir's regret over the 'emptiness in Soraya's womb' that 'seeped' into their marriage. In Amir's eyes, Soraya has failed. She is partly redeemed by the image of the 'mother she might have been' when she greets Sohrab. Faced with his withdrawal, she shifts into a 'holding pattern', to be restored to wholeness only when Sohrab is healed.

Rahim Khan

Quote

Come. There is a way to be good again.

Amir's mentor

Rahim Khan is Amir's spiritual father, indeed, Amir 'wishes he had been' his father. It is Rahim Khan whose finger the infant Amir grasps and he who 'rescues' Amir from Baba's withering scorn by offering to read his first story. Rahim Khan's encouragement and his gift of the leather-bound journal sustain Amir's literary aspirations in the face of his father's disapproval. He knows about Amir's betrayal of Hassan, yet does not judge him as harshly as Amir judges himself.

Most importantly, it is Rahim Khan who gives Amir 'a way to be good again' and who tells Amir of his blood relationship with Hassan. He also allows Amir to discover that he (Amir) and Baba were 'more alike' than Amir had ever realised. Finally, he skilfully orchestrates Amir's adoption of Sohrab, knowing intuitively that a relationship with Hassan's son will heal the wounds of the past. A wise and compassionate man, Rahim Khan is the guiding hand in Amir's quest for atonement.

Assef

Quote

Ethnic cleansing. I like it. I like the sound of it.

A symbol of evil

His admiration of Hitler casts Assef in the role of fascist maniac. Even as a child, when he terrorises Hazaras such as Hassan and Ali with racial abuse and physical violence, he is the archetype of evil. He has the oily charm of a hypocrite as he flatters Baba, and the sadistic instincts of a bully, using brass knuckles to win fights and revelling in the humiliation of Hassan, whom he brutally violates, and who must nonetheless respectfully serve him at Amir's party.

Assef matures into a 'sociopath', thrust into political power by the rise of the Taliban, whose ideology (superiority and racism) he adopts and whose methods (violence and murder) perfectly coincide with his own. Assef's paedophilia confirms him as unremittingly evil and symbolises the destructive relationship between the Taliban and vulnerable, disempowered people such as women and Hazaras.

General Taheri

Quote

People will ask. They will want to know why there is a Hazara boy living with our daughter.

The ageing patriarch

The 'general', as he is always called, symbolises the resilience of patriarchal values. He dominates his wife, suppressing her talents as a singer. He is driven by his paternal duty to protect the honour and chastity of his daughter, threatening to kill the man with whom she ran away. Ironically, it was precisely her father's heightened sense of paternal duty from which Soraya had fled. The general's raison d'être is firmly connected with his military status, even when it becomes irrelevant. He refuses to take a job 'unsuitable for a man of his stature' and lives on welfare payments, waiting for the day he can return to Afghanistan and resume a position of power.

General Taheri also perpetuates Afghan racial prejudices with his demeaning reference to Sohrab as a 'Hazara boy'. Despite his faults, the general is at heart, a good man, endeavouring to do the best for his family. Although his increasing frailty softens his relationship with Soraya, the general nonetheless represents the intolerance and inflexibility of patriarchal ideology.

Ali

Quote

Hassan was crying. Ali pulled him close, clutched him with tenderness.

Ali is to Baba what Hassan is to Amir. Orphaned as a child, Ali is adopted by Baba's father. His boyhood adventures with Baba foreshadow those of Hassan and Amir.

Baba's boyhood friend

Like his son, Ali is a gentle man, who endures racial abuse and the shame of his wife's desertion without complaint. His tender relationship with Hassan is juxtaposed (and contrasted) with Baba's rather heartless attitude to his son. During the shooting and explosions that signal the communist coup, Ali tenderly comforts his terrified son and Amir tells himself that he is 'not at all' envious. Amir's denial suggests that he would willingly trade his privileged life for the tenderness of a father like Ali.

Ali's 'cold, unforgiving look' in the face of Amir's lies and betrayal is the closest he ever comes to anger. His decision to leave Baba's household is a measure of both his deep disgust at Amir and his love for Hassan.

Farid

Quote

That's the real Afghanistan … You've always been a tourist here, you just didn't know it.

The fellow traveller

A minor but important character is Farid. Farid's role in Amir's 'quest' is a traditional one: the loyal follower whose support is integral to the 'hero's' success. Passionately patriotic and critical of those who have fled and return only to sell their properties, Farid initially regards Amir with hostility and suspicion. However, he is finally impressed by Amir's altruism and expresses his friendship in Hassan's words of loyalty: 'for you, a thousand times over'. Yet he is also a 'proud Pashtun', despite his poverty, and finds it difficult to believe that Amir would come 'all this way' for 'a Hazara boy.' His inability to accept Sohrab into his family indicates the depth of prejudice against Hazaras in Afghanistan.

Notes on Themes and Issues

Brotherhood, kinship and friendship

Quote

A kinship exists between people who've fed from the same breast.

Amir and Hassan's kinship

The novel's central theme, brotherhood, is closely examined through Amir's relationship with Hassan. Hosseini's central narrative of the brother who betrays a sibling and then redeems himself with love, shows how the idea of brotherhood, and the core values of loyalty and trust, underpin our social and personal relationships. The concept extends out and touches on related themes – particularly those of kinship (the general loyalty within families) and friendship (an extension of that blood bond).

Responsibility of brotherhood

Like brothers, Amir and Hassan share all their childhood experiences. Their friendship is expressed by the words on the pomegranate tree: 'Amir and Hassan, the Sultans of Kabul.' Their close comradeship, however, does not yet encompass true brotherhood as their values are radically different. Amir's condescension and jealousy contrast sharply with Hassan's absolute loyalty, most graphically demonstrated when Hassan is raped. Despite Amir's disloyalty and cowardice, Hassan's unwavering love creates a bond between them that transcends the ordinary boundaries of friendship.

'Real' brothers

Amir and Hassan's bond of brotherhood also arises from their shared parentage, literally, as it turns out, through Baba, and metaphorically through having fed 'from the same breast.' It is this 'blood' connection that forges the deeper bond as Amir looks at the polaroid photo of his brother's face. It is one of the novel's greatest surprises that the two are really blood brothers, as for almost two thirds of the narrative we are led to believe that the connection is symbolic. However, the 'blood' connection, 'powerful' as it might be, cannot be easily assumed to override the importance of the deeper bond (of love) between Amir and Hassan. Thus, while the betrayal (the rape incident and the subsequent lies) is even more appalling when seen in the light of Amir's blood connection to Hassan, it was already shocking enough to profoundly disturb the 'bad' brother. Amir, who betrayed the one who 'loved [him] in a way that no one ever had or would again.' 'Blood' ties serve to strengthen a relationship of brotherhood that already existed – even though Amir was too self-centred and arrogant to recognise it. Finally, the responsibilities of brotherhood compel Amir to sacrifice himself for Hassan – just as Hassan had done for him. Another step in the process of atonement is Amir's public declaration of his brotherhood with Hassan to Fadrid, Sohrab and finally to General Taheri. This is a poignant reminder of the words on the pomegranate tree which Amir finally stands by.

Racial divisions

Implicit in the author's exploration of brotherhood through personal relationships is a larger idea: one about universal brotherhood. The tribal divisions and racial hatreds that divide people are unequivocally condemned by Hosseini. Such divisions damage personal relationships and divide communities. More tragically, racial prejudice is at the basis of 'ethnic cleansing' and, most disturbingly, is deemed to be politically (and even morally) justifiable. The novel is unified in a strong argument for 'brotherhood' – or kinship, or friendship – or at the very least tolerance (treating others as you would want to be treated yourself). To this extent, its core theme is a timeless and universal one.

Betrayal and Redemption

Quote

I could step into that alley, stand up for Hassan …
Or I could run. In the end, I ran.
My body was broken … but I felt healed. Healed at last. I laughed.

Amir and Baba both betray childhood friends

Closely linked with the theme of brotherhood is that of betrayal. The betrayal of a brother or friend is a morally repugnant act and one of which Amir and Baba are both guilty. Baba's 'dishonouring' of Ali and Amir's 'sacrificing' of Hassan both have dreadful consequences. Baba cannot acknowledge a beloved son (Hassan). His relationship with Amir, whose legitimacy is a constant reminder of Hassan's illegitimacy, is initially an unsatisfying one for both father and son. Baba also betrays Amir, who finds out 'at the age of thirty-eight' that his whole life has been 'one big fucking lie.' Amir's guilty 'secret' gnaws at his conscience and invades his dreams, preventing him from becoming 'a man.'

Sohrab's lack of trust for the adult world

Just as Amir's trust in Baba and Rahim Khan is shattered by the revelation of their deceit, Sohrab's innocence is also destroyed by the corruption of the adult world. He is brutally orphaned by the Taliban soldiers, whose greed motivates the murder of his parents. He is betrayed (albeit unwillingly) by Zaman, the orphanage director, who 'sells' him to Assef. He is also betrayed by Amir, who makes him a promise that (at first) he cannot keep. Sohrab's suicide attempt is an act of despair by an innocent child who has been irrevocably damaged by a treacherous adult world.

Amir's redemption

Yet if betrayal causes terrible damage, there is also hope for redemption. Amir's difficult journey towards moral salvation is honestly told with no attempt to gloss over his cowardice and self-centredness. To attain redemption, Amir must think about others. His relationship with Soraya, and his final, much more considerate time with Baba, reveal Amir's capacity for emotional connection with others. But the real challenge is in coming to terms with the past, and specifically Hassan. That he goes to Pakistan is a sign that he is facing up to his guilt. That he accepts Rahim Khan's fearful challenge and goes after Sohrab, who must be rescued from a dangerously unstable and morally corrupt environment, is the next chapter in his redemption. Amir must confront physical danger, overcoming his cowardice – both moral and physical. He must openly admit and repent his sins, seeking forgiveness from those he has betrayed. His confession to Sohrab that he has done a 'lot of things [he] regrets in [his] life,' his 'profound' sorrow and his plea for 'forgiveness,' finally atones for his betrayal of Hassan – although Hassan's forgiveness had been already freely given.

Forgiveness

Forgiveness is essential to redemption, and Amir must also forgive himself. His brutal beating at the hands of Assef seems fitting. Amir is aptly punished for his sin and, through his suffering, is able to forgive the cowardly child who betrayed his closest friend. The ultimate attainment of Amir's redemption, however, is Sohrab's forgiveness. This does not come quite as easily as his father's had. Nevertheless, in the almost imperceptible 'curl' at 'the corner of Sohrab's mouth' is a subtle hope of Amir's redemption. It is not only his own redemption which Amir has gained – it is Baba's as well, as the illegitimate descendant of his 'dishonoured' Hazara servant is taken into the family of his legitimate Pashtun son. The act of redemption, therefore, is also one of reconciliation and has broader social implications for the divided nation of Afghanistan.

Father/son relationships

Quote

> I'd make a grand entrance, a hero, the prized trophy in my bloodied hands. The old warrior would walk to the young one, embrace him and acknowledge his worthiness.

Paternal expectations

The weight of paternal expectations is often overwhelming. Driven by a need to prove himself, Baba outshines his father, a 'respected judge', with his feats of daring and the accumulation of wealth and power. Amir struggles to prove himself, burdened by his sense of inadequacy and intimidated by his father's 'towering' physical presence. The story of 'Shahnamah' (a Persian epic), has a particular resonance for Amir. The words: 'If thou art indeed my father, then thou hast stained thy sword in the life-blood of thy son,' metaphorically express Amir's bitterness at his father's rejection. Amir's desperate need to 'bring [the kite] home and show Baba … once and for all that his son was worthy,' is Amir's only hope of securing the affection he craves.

Ali and Hassan

Juxtaposed with the difficult relationship between Baba and Amir is that between Ali and Hassan. Ali is a gentle and loving father, cradling in his arms the disfigured, newborn infant, despite his certain knowledge that he could not be the father of the child. The importance of 'blood' is overridden by the depth of paternal affection Ali feels for Hassan. Ironically, it is the importance of 'blood' that awakens Baba's paternal affection for the son he cannot acknowledge. Baba, however, scrupulously fulfils his responsibilities to both his sons. He 'never forgets' Hassan's birthday, and sacrifices his own happiness to provide a better future in America for Amir.

As he matures, Amir's relationship with Baba improves, partly because Baba finds a reason to be proud of him, but also because Baba mellows with age and is able to acknowledge his tenderness for his son. The paternal relationship which sustains Amir through his childhood, however, is with Rahim Khan. It is Rahim who reasons with Baba, chiding him over his harsh treatment of Amir, and it is he who nurtures Amir's talent for writing. Rahim Khan also takes paternal responsibility for Amir's moral guidance, gently insisting that he finds 'a way to be good again.'

The theme is central to the novel. Hosseini has shown us a 'bad' father (Baba) and two 'good' fathers (Ali and Rahim Khan – the surrogate). He has demonstrated the ways the critical attitudes of the former withers and how the love and support of the latter is enhanced. He has also shown us a symbolic father, Amir himself (re Sohrab), and the way he can, with enlightenment, become the good father. He also shows the result: Amir's affection and patience finally pay off in the novel's celebratory ending.

Religious faith

Quote

And they call themselves Muslim.

For most of its length, *The Kite Runner* appears to take a dim view of organised religion – in this case Islam. We recall Baba's contempt for the 'self-righteous monkeys' (the mullahs) at the Islamic school. Amir seems to have a similarly sceptical view. He even passes the time with Farid cracking anti-mullah jokes.

The extremism of the Taliban

With the shocking chapters set in Kabul under the Taliban, Hosseini's horror at religious extremism is palpable. The scene in the stadium, for instance, where the adulterous man and woman are stoned to death under Sharia law, is one of the two most savage in the novel (along with the rape scene). Assef is a figure of unthinkable evil, and in-so-far as he becomes the embodiment of the Taliban, we cannot escape the conclusion that here is religion at its most perverted.

Yet, in the aftermath of Sohrab's suicide attempt, Amir desperately seeks comfort (and hope) in his faith. He effectively converts, and stays converted. There is no further criticism of the faith at all.

What looks like a strange U-turn is in fact a way of making a point. It coincides with and parallels Amir's own inner growth as he redeems himself. The novel is basically about moral problems – about the problem of being 'good'. Is goodness guaranteed by outward religious observance? Of course not. That is clear from the fatuous mullahs and the murderous Taliban. These men, despite their professions of moral rectitude, are inwardly weak, if not evil. Goodness comes from within, from a commitment to good acts, compassion, loyalty, and selflessness.

Yet, and this is a point he is making quite deliberately, religion is far from irrelevant. The yearning for God, for forgiveness, for a clear conscience, is natural, he seems to be arguing. That urge *is* compatible with organised religion. The comfort that Amir finds in his traditional faith in his 'hour of need' can be taken as a sign from the author that religion does have a place. Just as the text overall argues for morality, Amir's own conversion points to a spiritual need in people. We may rightly reject lunatic excesses claimed in the name of religion (the Taliban), but the faith itself is not so easily rejected. Hosseini is not even making so unsubtle a point that there are good Muslims and bad Muslims. He is pointing out that religion points to the essential moral core in life, without which, he believes, we are incomplete. It might be worth , however, questioning an implicit assumption that there is a *necessary* connection between religious faith and moral goodness.

What the Critics Say

[Hosseini evokes] through powerful storytelling, a feeling of what it is like to be an Afghan, to see one's beautiful country destroyed, to live in fear. The author is able to depict moral complexities without clunkiness, instead catching the breath, and heart, of the reader. Because of this skill, I feel he is able to do risky things with both character and plot, so that any occasional moment where the reader's credulity could be stretched turns out to be a moment of immensely satisfying narrative pleasure. (Sue Bond, www.reviewsofbooks.com/kite_runner).

Hosseini's narrative is fast-paced, and his sensitive portrayal of childhood with all its fears and tensions is particularly striking. The glimpses of Afghan family life and values are captivating, particularly because they have been virtually unknown in American fiction, but it is the author's focus on the humanity of the characters that gives the novel its universality and great appeal. Amir's betrayal of Hassan is believable and understandable in human terms, apart from culture, and his long-term remorse is not surprising. Hassan's nobility in the face of his trauma, born from both his unwavering acceptance of his role as a servant and his genuine affection for Amir, gives him a saintly aspect which never cloys—he has simply accepted the role he's been given in life. (Mary Whipple, www.mostlyfiction.com/world/hosseini.htm).

Some of the plot's turns and twists may be somewhat implausible, but Hosseini has created characters that seem so real that one almost forgets that *The Kite Runner* is a novel and not a memoir. At a time when Afghanistan has been thrust into the forefront of America's collective consciousness ("people sipping lattes at Starbucks were talking about the battle for Kunduz"), Hosseini offers an honest, sometimes tragic, sometimes funny, but always heartfelt view of a fascinating land. Perhaps the only true flaw in this extraordinary novel is that it ends all too soon. (Gisele Toueg, www.reviewsofbooks.com/kite_runner).

The character studies alone would make this a noteworthy debut, from the portrait of the sensitive, insecure Amir to the multilayered development of his father, Baba, whose sacrifices and scan-

dalous behaviour are fully revealed only when Amir returns to Afghanistan and learns the true nature of his relationship to Hassan. Add an incisive, perceptive examination of recent Afghan history and its ramifications in both America and the Middle East, and the result is a complete work of literature that succeeds in exploring the culture of a previously obscure nation that has become a pivot point in the global politics of the new millennium. (© 2003 Reed Business Information, Inc.
www.reviewsofbooks.com/kite_runner).

Writing an Exam Essay

1 Topic analysis

Your essential starting point for writing a quality answer is topic analysis. Look carefully at the words in the question. For example:

'Despite his courage in rescuing Sohrab, Amir is essentially a self-centred character who never fully redeems himself.'

What are the key words? What is the basic concept of the topic? Here it is that Amir is 'self-centred' and most importantly that he never 'redeems' himself. The word 'redeems' is not only a lead into the novel's central moral argument, (about how people should behave) it actually needs discussing in its own right. What is it? How does it fit the character?

The topic offers you a negative view of the protagonist. You do not have to agree! You can argue that he is a good person, and that he does undo his childhood 'sin'. There is no 'right' answer. You must find your own opinion, and express it.

2 Planning

On the basis of your analysis, make detailed notes on each of the key words and ideas. Think of quotes to go with your ideas. Make connections between different issues.

3 Paragraphing

Now allocate the major ideas/issues to a set of paragraphs. Your introductory paragraph (1) should show you understand the topic. Don't just repeat the question – paraphrase it cleverly, with examples from the text. State your point of view – do you accept the topic argument, or not? Paragraphs 2 – 4 (or 5) then discuss each major aspect of the topic. Make sure each one has a **topic sentence** (normally the first). The last paragraph is your conclusion – sum up the key issues, and restate your point of view neatly.

4 Writing and revision

You should now (because of your planning) find writing the essay easy. You are just writing from your notes. Don't forget to revise quickly for errors (spelling, grammar, etc), before finishing.

Sample Essays

Essay 1

Despite his courage in rescuing Sohrab, Amir is essentially a self-centred character who never fully redeems himself.

Discuss.

Introduction considers the focus of the topic and sets up the main contention.

As a child Amir is often selfish, disloyal and cowardly. As he matures, he often thinks more of himself than others, and his decision to rescue Sohrab is arrived at only after considerable pressure from Rahim Khan. When he does agree, it could be argued that it is because of a need to feel 'good' about himself rather than genuine concern for the son of his childhood friend. Despite this, Amir eventually displays great courage in facing up to a dangerous and sadistic bully. He comes to care deeply about the damaged child and, in repaying the debt of loyalty he owes to Hassan, Amir finally makes amends for his shameful behaviour. In doing so, he atones, not only for his own sins, but also those of his father.

Topic sentence 'looks back' to the main topic and 'looks forward' to the main idea to be developed in the paragraph.

Amir has much to atone for in his quest for redemption. His 'idyllic' childhood is spent with Hassan, whose absolute loyalty is the one thing Amir can rely on. Despite the fact that Amir refers to Hassan as his 'servant' rather than his 'friend', Hassan stands up to the bully, Assef, courageously defending Amir. More shameful is Amir's failure to stand up for Hassan, leaving him to the mercy of Assef, who brutally rapes him. It might be argued that Baba's 'hardness' is partly to blame for Amir's unacceptable behaviour. Hassan becomes 'the price' Amir '[has] to pay to win Baba.' Nevertheless, when the adult Amir no longer needs to compete for Baba's affections, his behaviour is still often selfish and thoughtless. When Baba is diagnosed with terminal cancer and refuses chemotherapy, Amir's characteristically self-centred response is: 'What about me … What am I supposed to do?' Amir's selfishness, cowardice and treachery are deeply entrenched, overcoming his failings is crucial to his redemption.

Rahim Khan's telephone call offers Amir 'a way to be good again.' Despite his enduring self-disgust, Amir does not readily

Amir's reluctance to accept the opportunity for redemption

embrace his opportunity for salvation. He resists the pleas of Rahim Khan to go to Kabul and rescue Sohrab, offering to 'pay someone [else] to go.' Rahim's angry response '... we both know why it has to be you,' emphasises Amir's guilt, yet Amir again thinks of himself, his 'wife in America, [his] home ... career ... family.' This, again, is abject cowardice and shameful self-interest, and Amir is clearly not yet significantly different from the spineless child who betrayed his loyal friend. Rahim's 'best card' – a plea to 'grant an old man his dying wish' – is not enough to sway Amir who 'toys with [his] wedding ring' and accuses Rahim of thinking 'too highly' of him. Amir's willingness to *admit* to being a coward rather than grant the dying wish of his 'mentor' and loyal supporter again reveals just how cowardly he is. Appeals to Amir's better nature are ineffective and Rahim Khan must provide Amir with a more compelling reason to rescue Sohrab. Yet when Rahim informs Amir of the blood relationship he shares with Sohrab, Amir first thinks of himself. He 'storms' out of the apartment, thinking only that his life has been 'one big fucking lie.' If he is to redeem himself, Amir must overcome, not only the dangers awaiting him in Kabul, but also a tendency to wallow in his self-disgust, which is easier than confronting his fears.

Amir becomes less selfish and more courageous but might still be motivated by self-interest.

Amir's slow journey towards salvation begins when he looks at the polaroid photo Rahim Khan has given him and sees his 'brother's face'– the face of a person who had loved him 'in a way that no one ever had or would again.' On one level, it could be argued that this is also about Amir whose 'blood' connection with Sohrab renders him worthy of rescuing. On another level, however, Amir begins to recognise the debt of gratitude he owes to someone whose love and loyalty he took entirely for granted and shamefully exploited. A significant turning point in Amir's moral development occurs at the hotel near Pashtunistan Square where he and Farid share a meal. Farid's incredulity that Amir would 'come all the way from America ... for a Shi'a' deeply offends Amir, who as a child, had told himself that Hassan was 'just a Hazara' while he watched him being raped by Assef. Amir's ability to transcend his deeply ingrained racial prejudices is admirable, and is certainly a redeeming quality, and his determination to find Sohrab, despite having to venture into a dangerous Taliban stronghold is extremely courageous. What is still open to question, however, is whether Amir's need to feel 'good again' can be construed as self-interest.

The line between self-interest and altruism is crossed as Amir risks his life.

As Amir finally confronts Assef, he also confronts his own cowardice and betrayal. With his 'snarl … spit-shining teeth and [rolling] bloodshot eyes,' Assef becomes Amir's 'black bear', and Amir is as brave as Baba once was, but without Baba's considerable physical strength. During the savage beating inflicted on him, Amir begins to laugh uncontrollably. This is an echo of the 'relief' felt by Assef himself as his kidney stones were dislodged during a beating from a prison guard. For Amir, the relief is from the shameful burden of his past, he feels 'healed at last.' This is essential for his redemption because it enables Amir to shift his focus from the guilt that has consumed him and think about Sohrab's needs. Amir also repays Hassan by saving his son, and atones for the sins of Baba, who had also betrayed his childhood friend by dishonouring him in 'the single worst way [for] an Afghan man.' Sohrab's fleeting smile after the kite contest in the park suggests the possibility of further 'healing.' Sohrab's ability to trust can be restored through his relationship with Amir; it is this trust which finally redeems Amir.

Conclusion reminds the reader of the main point of the argument.

Given that Amir is initially so self-centred and cowardly, his act of courage and self-sacrifice is commendable. Redemption is not easily achieved for Amir, but ultimately, he makes the choice he has to make. In saving Hassan's son, Amir has become the 'old warrior' of the Afghan legend who can at last acknowledge his own 'worthiness'. The final image of Amir running, with 'the wind blowing in [his] face … and a smile as wide as the Valley of Panjsher' suggests that whatever Amir has suffered to achieve redemption, it was worth the cost.

Essay 2

'*The Kite Runner*' shows that no matter how deeply the past is buried, it will 'claw its way out.'

Discuss.

Introduction considers the importance of the past

Khaled Hosseini's semi-autobiographical novel opens with the words, 'I became what I am today at the age of twelve.' It is immediately apparent that Amir, the protagonist, is reflecting on a troubled past; one which he might have 'buried' but cannot forget. In trying to forget, Amir is in danger of forever remaining a cowardly child, living with a gnawing feeling of self-disgust. Amir's shameful past does indeed 'claw its way out' and, to his credit, he eventually faces up to the unresolved issues which have troubled his dreams. Yet sometimes the past *is* better buried. The cultural divisions which plague Afghanistan's troubled history need to be left behind if the country, like the protagonist, is to be 'healed.'

Topic sentence 'looks back' to the main topic. This paragraph develops an argument about the impossibility of forgetting the past

After his betrayal of Hassan, Amir almost immediately begins to bury the past. He returns in triumph with the vanquished blue kite and basks in the warmth of Baba's embrace. In Baba's arms, Amir 'forgot what [he'd] done. And it was good.' In order to suppress his feelings of shame and guilt, Amir projects his self-loathing onto his friend, calling Hassan a 'coward' and pelting him with pomegranates. Smeared in red (an ominous portent of his eventual fate) Hassan picks up a pomegranate and crushes it against his own forehead, asking Amir if he feels 'better.' Amir has become the 'monster' of Hassan's dream, who 'dragged' him to the 'murky bottom' of the lake. As an adult, Amir seems to have successfully buried his past. He graduates from college and begins to develop his skills as a writer. He marries Soraya and has his first novel published. To outward appearances, Amir is the success his father had so desperately wished for. Yet his sleepless nights and troubled dreams reveal the inescapable burden of a past which Amir cannot forget.

Amir's past dramatically re-emerges in the voice of Rahim Khan, whose quiet insistence forces Amir to return to Afghanistan. In reminding Amir of his moral duty to Hassan, Rahim Khan uncovers unpleasant aspects of Baba's long-buried past. Baba's dalliance with the wife of his childhood friend was a 'shameful situation'

This paragraph responds to the topic's invitation to consider a wider range of characters (not just Amir)

which could have irrevocably damaged Baba's honour. Rahim Khan is 'ashamed' of the lies in which he was complicit. His own buried past must be laid bare before he dies and Amir's 'forgiveness' must be sought. Baba's past indiscretion, although very carefully concealed is never forgotten by Baba. He becomes a 'tortured soul' whose 'socially legitimate' son is a constant reminder to Baba of his shame and guilt. Baba's harshness with Amir becomes a way for Baba to punish himself for his sins, just as Amir had punished Hassan, and just as Amir's guilt plagues him as an adult, the cancer that eventually destroys Baba can be seen as a symbol of his enduring guilt. Baba's refusal to undergo chemotherapy, and his defiant smoking, suggest that he embraces his fate as a fitting punishment for his sin of burying his past.

Some aspects of the past need to be buried – particularly the double standards relating to men's and women's rights

While there are some aspects of the past that cannot be buried, there are clearly those that should be. Soraya's past indiscretion is not forgotten, and 'a whisper here, an insinuation there' send Soraya's prospective suitors fleeing 'like startled birds.' At a cousin's wedding, after hearing two middle-aged women agreeing that the groom 'did well' not to marry her, Soraya breaks down, complaining bitterly that men can 'get their girlfriends pregnant and no one says a god-damn thing,' but she makes 'one mistake' and pays for it 'for the rest of [her] life.' Another woman whose past continues to haunt her is Sanaubar. Burdened by her 'dishonourable' reputation, Sanaubar is forced into an unsuitable marriage with Ali, a much older man who is sterile and partly crippled. Sanaubar's past haunts not only Sanaubar herself, but also her son, who is the victim of crude taunts about his mother. As an old woman, Sanaubar returns to the son she has abandoned to seek his forgiveness and it a measure of Hassan's generosity of spirit that he can bury the past by forgiving his mother and welcoming her into his family. Hassan also buries the pain of Amir's betrayal, remembering only his love for Amir, and telling Sohrab that Amir was 'the best friend' he ever had. Clearly, there are times when burying the past is the right thing to do.

It is not only Sanaubar's tarnished reputation that society will not bury, it is also her Hazara status. Her ragged and battered appearance when she arrives on Hassan's doorstep suggests that life has not been easy for an outcast Hazara woman with a disreputable past. The traditional discrimination against the Hazaras is centuries old and divides Afghans into the privileged and the oppressed and even close friendships are marred by

Racial discrimination is also an aspect of the past which needs to be buried

racial prejudice. Although Amir treats Hassan 'like a friend … more like a brother,' his attitude changes when Baba's friends come to visit with their children and Hassan is never included in their games. Amir is quick to deny his friendship when challenged by Assef, referring to Hassan as his 'servant,' not his 'friend.' It is only when he has finally faced up to his own past that Amir is able to disregard the Hazara status of Hassan's son, adopting him as a son and chastising his father-in-law for his thoughtless comment about a 'Hazara boy.'

Conclusion refocuses on the topic and reaffirms the argument

The Kite Runner is a moving account of a return to the past. Through the painful journey of Amir, Hosseini shows that the effects of the past are enduring; they can damage relationships and destroy lives. Sometimes, however, it is simply not enough to remember past actions, it is often necessary to step back into a past life and fight the battles that were avoided. Sometimes, too, the prejudices of the past must be laid to rest, and Amir's ability to do this offers a glimmer of hope that racial tensions in Afghanistan might one day be replaced by greater tolerance.

Sample Essay Questions

1. 'Amir is not the only one who cannot admit the truth.'

   Discuss.

2. 'It is Hassan rather than Amir who is the true hero of *The Kite Runner*.'

   Discuss.

3. 'Amir is selfish and cowardly, but he is not entirely to blame for his flaws.'
   Discuss.

4. 'Despite Amir's good intentions, Sohrab has been damaged too badly; he will never fully recover.'

   Discuss.

5. 'Although the women are always in the background, they are stronger than the men.'

   Discuss.

6. 'Troubled times bring out the best and the worst in people.'

   Discuss.

7. 'Kinship is the strongest of all human relationships.'

   Discuss.

8. 'It is the experiences of childhood that determine who we will become.'

   Discuss.

Titles in this series so far

The Accidental Tourist
The Age of Innocence
Angela's Ashes
Antigone
Away and the Journey
Baghdad Blog
Border Crossing
Brave New World / Blade Runner
Briar Rose
Brilliant Lies
The Brush-Off
Cabaret
The Chant of Jimmie Blacksmith
Cloudstreet
The Collector
Cosi
The Curious Incident of the Dog in the Night-time
Dispossessed
The Divine Wind
Diving for Pearls
Educating Rita
Emma & Clueless
Falling
Fine Line
Fly Away Peter
Follow Your Heart
The Freedom of the City
Frontline
Gattaca
Generals Die in Bed
Girl with a Pearl Earring
Going Home
Great Expectations
The Great Gatsby
Hamlet
The Handmaid's Tale
Henry Lawson's Stories
I for Isobel
If His is a Man
An Imaginary Life
I'm not scared
In Between
In Country
In the Lake of the Woods
Inheritance
The Inheritors
The Journey Area of Study
King Lear
The Kitchen God's Wife
Kite Runner
Lantana
A Lesson before Dying
Letters from the Inside
The Life and Crimes of Harry Lavender
Lionheart
Looking for Alibrandi
The Lost Salt Gift of Blood
Macbeth
Maestro
A Man for All Seasons
Medea
Montana 1948
My Left Foot
My Name is Asher Lev
My Place
Night
No Great Mischief
Oedipus Rex
One True Thing
Othello
The Outsider
Paper Nautilus
The Plague
The Player
Pride and Prejudice
The Quiet American
Rabbit-Proof Fence
Raw
Schindler's List
Shakespeare in Love
The Shipping News
Sometimes Gladness
Stolen
Strictly Ballroom
Things Fall Apart
Tirra Lirra by the River
The Truman Show
A View from the Bridge
We All Fall Down
The Wife of Martin Guerre
Wild Cat Falling
Witness